typ◯gr▲phics pl▲y&w◯rk

2D ☞ 3D

タイポグラフィの現在進行形

BNN
Bug News Network

Copyright © 2011 by BNN, Inc.

Published by
BNN, Inc.
21 Arai Building, 1-20-6, Ebisu-minami,
Shibuya-ku, Tokyo, 150-0022, Japan
Mail: info@bnn.co.jp

Cover Designed by
Kitayama Masakazu (HELP!)

Editors
Yusuke Shouno, Natsumi Fujita, Tomoya Yoshida
Translated by
Natsumi Fujita, Ryutaro Uchiyama, Joowhan Suh, Go Hirose

ISBN 978-4-86100-770-5
Printed in Japan by SHINANO CO., LTD.

凡例:
作品キャプションは
「タイトル／カテゴリー／クライアント／制作年度／クレジット」
の順番で記している。

explanatory notes
RDV Design (Ttitle)
Illustration, Set Design (Categry) / Edition Infopresse (Cliant) /
2000 (Production Year)
Art Direction: Julien de repentigny (Credit)

chapter

〔 空 間 に あ る 文 字 〕

2次元から3次元へ。

紙上から飛び出して、空間の中で切り開かれつつあるタイポグラフィの新しい地平。

CGによるオブジェクトから、空間を利用したスカルプチャー、そしてアナログなハンドメイドまで、

多種多様な3Dのタイポグラフィを紹介する。

From two dimensions to three.

Typography leaps out of the sheet of paper into the spatial domain, opening up a new horizon.

We introduce various manifestations of 3D typography,

from sculptural works occupying space to the analog and the handmade.

1

3 dimensional

typgraphy

RDV Design
Illustration, Set Design / Edition Infopresse /
2000
Design: Julien de repentigny

Logo Brochure Branding
Illustration, Set Design / Computer Arts
Magazine / 2000

Design: Julien de repentigny,
Photography: Leda & St-Jacques

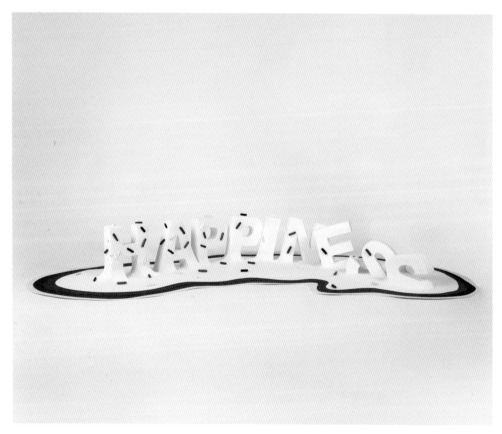

MILK
Package Design / Self-Initiated / 2000
Design: Julien de repentigny

Paper Type Serie
Illustration, Montage / Self-Initiated / 2000
Design: Julien de repentigny

3 Dimensional Typography

Down with the Crown
Event Branding / Orange Ski Apparel / 2000
Design: Julien de repentigny

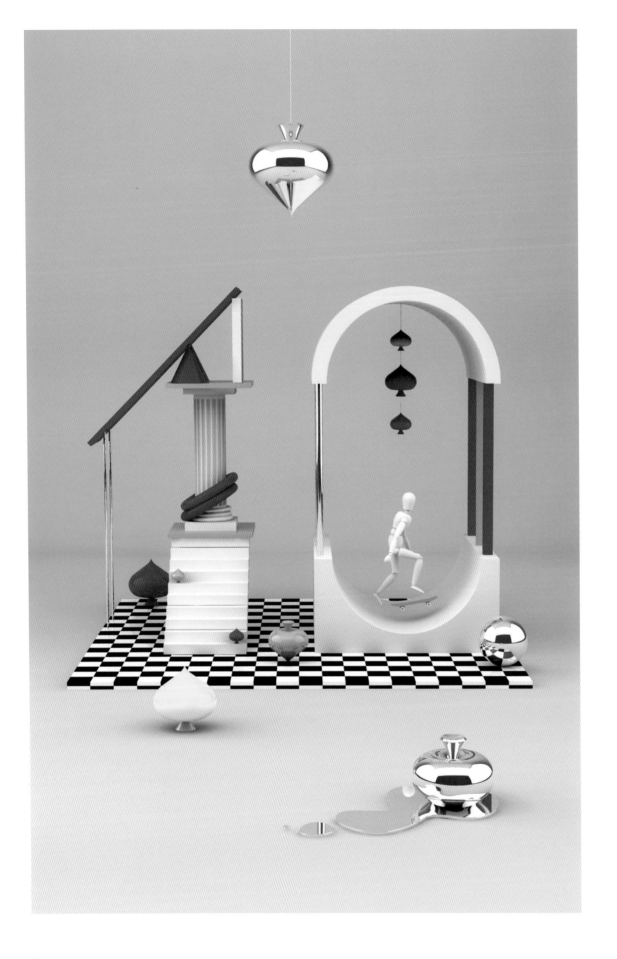

10
Cards / Lovit Store / 2010
Design: Pablo Alfieri

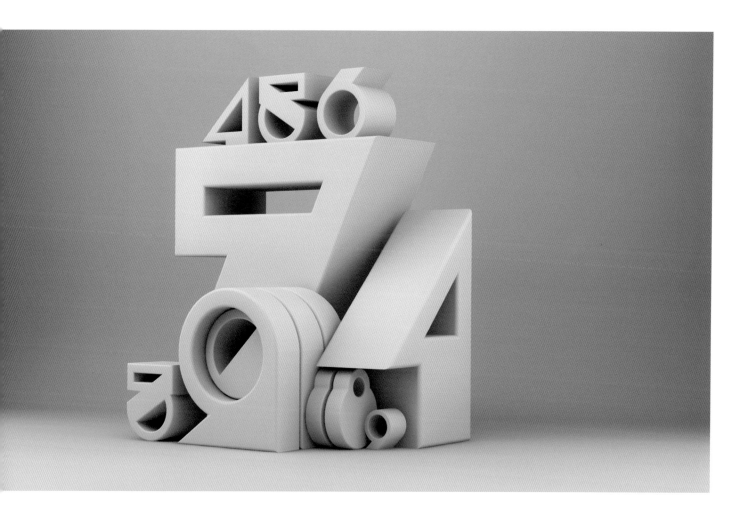

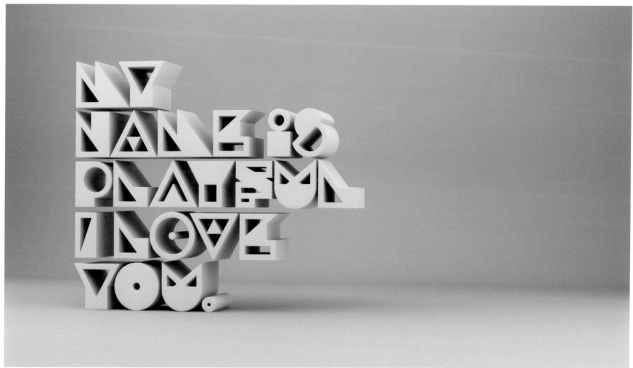

PLAYFUL TYPE
Self Promotional / 2011
Design: Pablo Alfieri

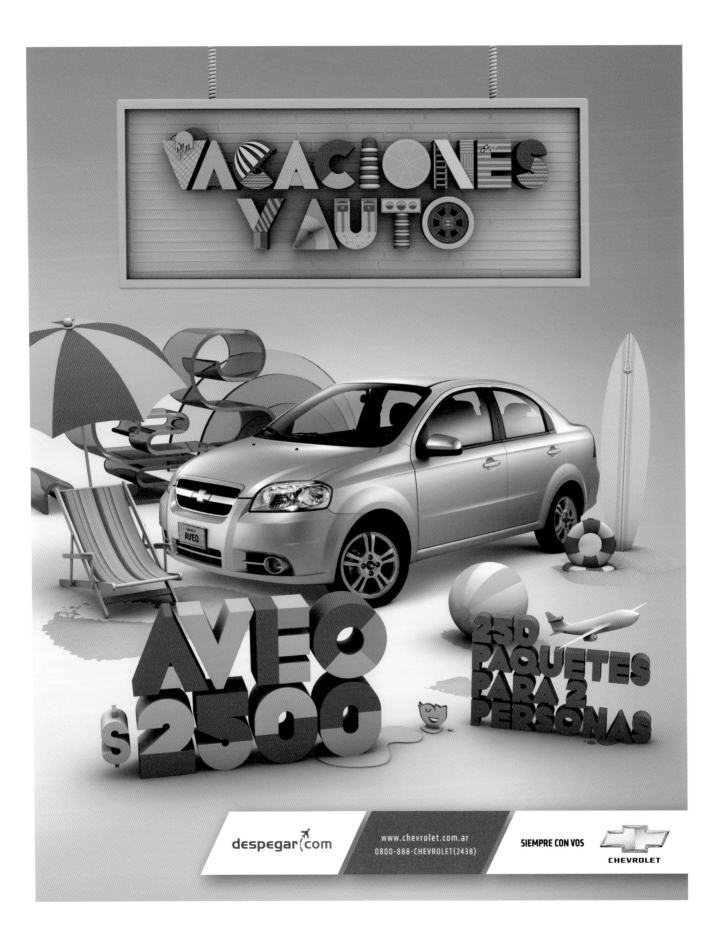

CHEVROLET
TV Commercials and Print Campaign / General
Motors / 2009
Design: Pablo Alfieri

GANCIA ONE
Billboard and TV commercials / Cepas
Argentinas / 2010
Design: Pablo Alfieri

3 Dimensional Typography

Raking Leaves in the wind
Poster for the exhibition / 2008
Art Direction+Design: Julien Vallée,
Eve Duhamel, Brent Wadden

Tangible – Hi touch visuals
Cover Art for Tangible / Gestalten Verlag / 2008
Art direction+Design: Julien Vallée,
Photography: Simon Duhamel

MTV One
Image Proposition for MTV-One / MTV-One / 2008
Art Direction: Julien Vallée + Dixon Baxi,
Design: Julien Vallée

YCN – A is for Award
Artwork / YCN / 2009
Art Direction+Design: Julien Vallée,
Photography: Simon Duhamel

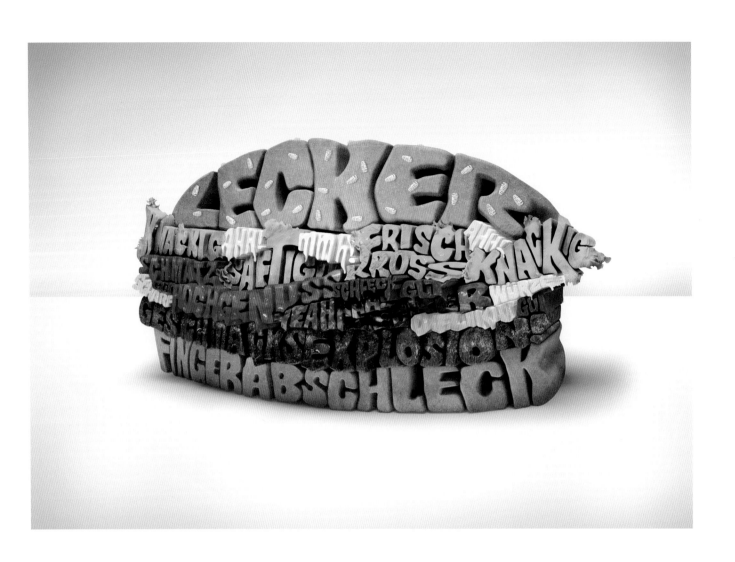

Typoburger
Advertisement / Burger King Germany / 2010
Design: Serial Cut ™ , 3D Artist: Jimmy Andersson

3 Dimensional Typography

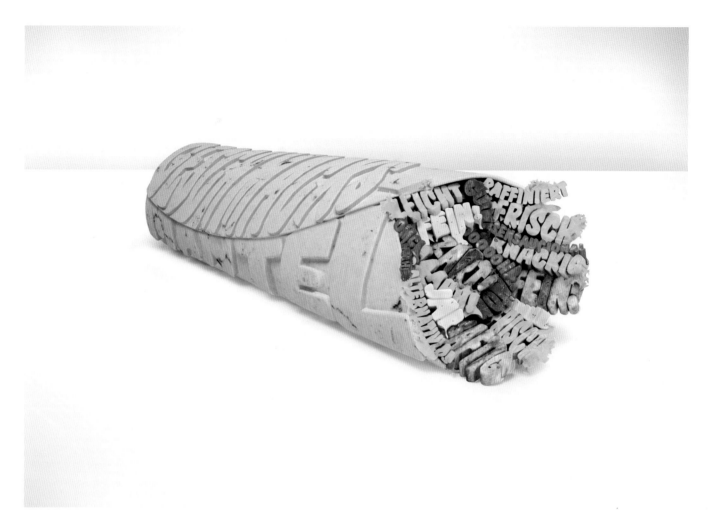

Icon
Poster / Self Promotion / 2011
Design: Serial Cut ™,
Photography: Paloma Rincón

Ideal
Poster / Self Promotion / 2010
Design: Serial Cut ™,
Photography: Paloma Rincón

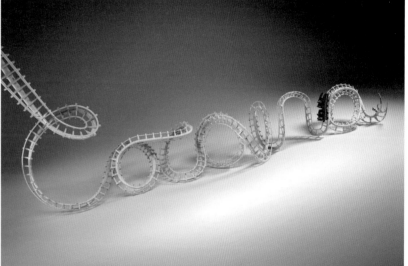

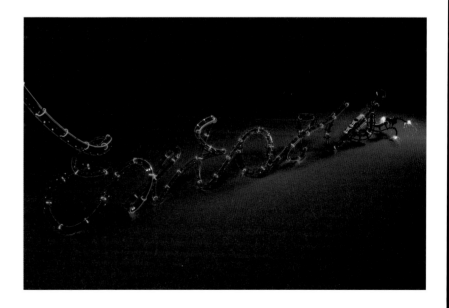

Druggercoasters
Advertisement / FAD Anti Drug Association / 2011
Design: Serial Cut ™ , 3D Artist: Jimmy Andersson

Jamon
Poster / ICEX London / 2010
Design: Serial Cut ™, 3D artist: Jimmy
Andersson

Rockoil
Poster / Self Promotion / 2010
Design: Serial Cut ™, 3D artist: Jimmy
Andersson

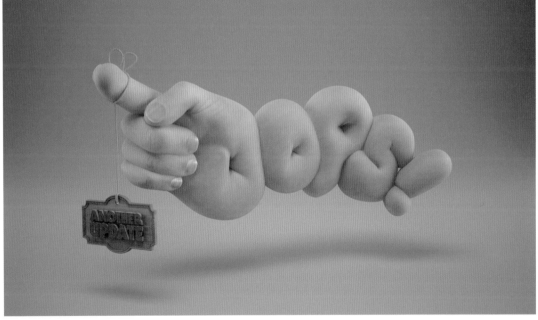

Antena 3 Films
Logotype / Antena 3 Films / 2011
Design: Serial Cut ™

Oops!
Poster / Self Promotion / 2011
Design: Serial Cut ™, 3D artist: Jimmy
Andersson

Zune Marketplace
Advertisement / Zune / 2009

Design: Serial Cut ™

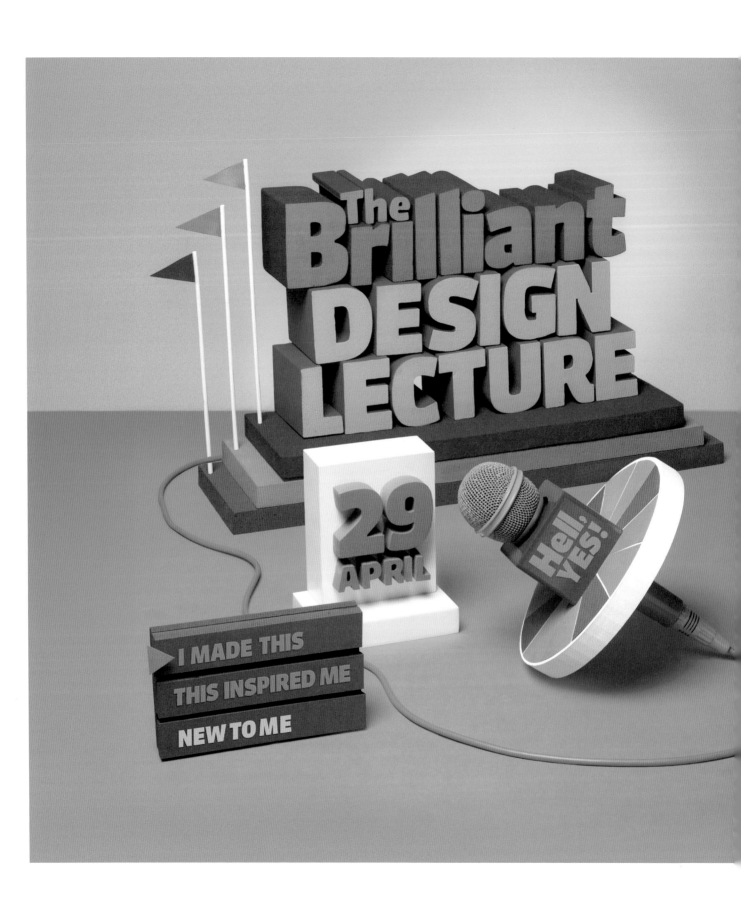

TBDL - The Brilliant Design Lecture
Advertisement / University of Huddersflield / 2010
Design: Serial Cut ™ , Photography: Paloma Rincón

3 Dimensional Typography

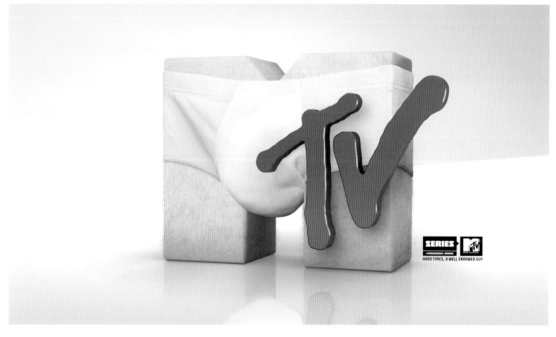

The Colors
Advertisement / Jotun / 2011
Design: Serial Cut ™,
Photography: Paloma Rincón

Hard Times
Logotype / MTV / 2011
Design: Serial Cut ™

ME 002
Picture for a poster of a electronic music festival
/ Mercredi Production / 2011
Design: Akatre

Space for Fantasy
Picture for a contemporary art exhibition /
Galeries Lafayette / 2010
Design: Akatre

Kids Alphabet (Bon Voyage)
Original Work / 2008

Visual: NAM, Art Direction: Takayuki Nakazawa,
Photography: Hiroshi Manaka,
Photo Retouching: Yoshiaki Sakurai

"D", "R", "E", "A", "M"
DIGITAL TEMPLE MAGAZINE / 2009

Visual: NAM, Art Direction: Takayuki Nakazawa,
Photography: Hiroshi Manaka

Photo Retouching: Yoshiaki Sakurai, Styling:
Atsushi Kimura, Hair: Chieko Ishizuka
Make-up: Akii, Model: ARI (eva management)

Marry Me Project / No days off
Photography / Self-Initiation / 2008
Design and Photography: Ethan Park

3 Dimensional Typography

Marry Me Project / Hugs for you
Photography / Self-Initiation / 2008
Design and Photography: Ethan Park

Marry Me Project / Let's share
Photography / Self-Initiation / 2008
Design and Photography: Ethan Park

June Issue
Magazine Calendar Cover design / Fast
Company Magazine / 2010
Design and Photography: Ethan Park

...mentre la TV registra quello che vuoi tu.

Da oggi sei libero. Sei libero di non avere più limiti. Sei tu a decidere quando è troppo presto, quando è già tardi, quando è davvero il momento giusto per i tuoi programmi preferiti. Puoi vedere quello che vuoi, quanto e quando vuoi, per dare alle tue passioni sempre lo spazio che meritano. Con la tecnologia all'avanguardia che solo My Sky HD ti offre, non ci sono programmi che contano più dei tuoi.
Chiama 02.7070 o vai su sky.it

sky
Liberi di...

...quello che ti piace di più in TV.

Da oggi sei libero. Sei libero di non accontentarti. In ogni momento se vuoi puoi trovare qualcosa per cui ridere, piangere, tifare fino a perdere la voce, tornare bambino e riscoprire il gusto di esplorare. Tutto questo grazie all'offerta unica di oltre 200 canali di cinema, sport, calcio, serie tv, intrattenimento, cartoni animati, lifestyle, documentari, musica e news: solo su Sky quello che cerchi non è mai diverso da quello che trovi.
Chiama 02.7070 o vai su sky.it

sky
Liberi di...

SKY TV Re-branding Campaign
Advertisement for prints, billboards, posters, and
Web / Sky TV Italy / 2010

Art director: Ethan Park, Art Coordinator: Dino
Allladin, Photography: Daniel Jon

Ethan Park Marry me Project
Looking for talent in a woman from 21 to 23 Oct. 2008
@ Barge House Street London United KingdomSE1 9PH RSVP on 07885 710 806

How I can touch your heart
Poster series / Self-Initiation / 2008
Design and Photography: Ethan Park,
Copywriter: Louise Shepherd

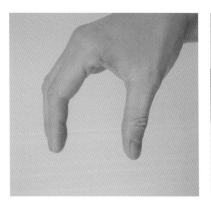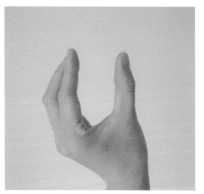

Neutral / 2009
Design: Wonder Wonder

Vegetableplay letters / 2009
Design: Wonder Wonder

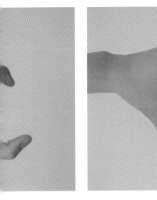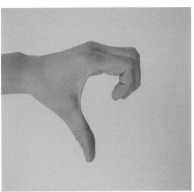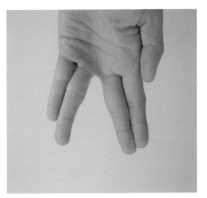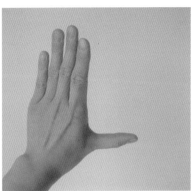

Cafe De Chill / 2009
Design: Wonder Wonder

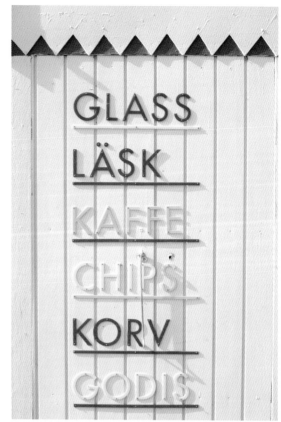

P●PCORN 20

SOCKERVADD 2●

CHIPS 15

KORV M.BRÖD 15

FRENCH HOTDOG 23

PANNKAK●R M.SYLT 28*

*GLASS ELLER GRÄDDE

Kiosk graphic identity
People's Park in Malmö / 2009
Art Direction: Byggstudio (Hanna Nilsson &
Sofia Østerhus)

3 Dimensional Typography

People's Park Notice Board
People's Park in Malmö / 2009-2010
Art Direction: Byggstudio (Hanna Nilsson &
Sofia Østerhus)

OF ALL THE
THINGS

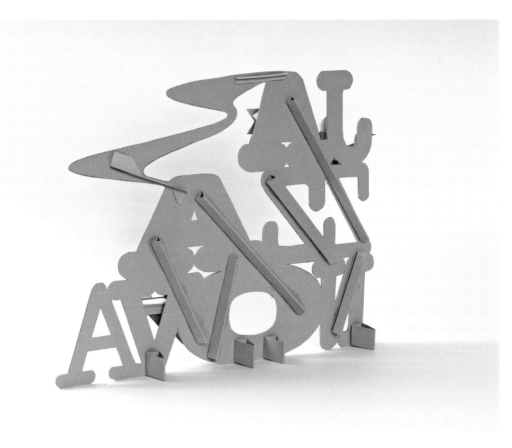

Jazzanova
CD, LP Cover Artwork / Universal Music / 2009
Design: HORT

3 Dimensional Typography

Stop
Posters / Doing Boundless Exhibition / 2010
Design: HORT, Build together by Michael Burmann

No Titlle
Digital printing, Billboard / Installation / 2009
Design: Tim Rehm and Tim Sürken @ HORT

Two of our longtime Hort members, Tim Rehm & Tim Sürken, presented some of their work at Marta Herford Museum. The installation, which was specially developed for the exhibition "hier und anderswo", deals with the transience in global internet communications.

我々の Hort の長期のメンバーである Tim Rehm と Tim Sürken は作品の幾つかをマルタ・ヘルフォード・美術館で展示した。『Hier Und Anderswo』のために特別に製作されたインスタレーションは、グローバルなインターネット・コミュニケーションの移ろいやすさをテーマとして取り扱っている。

"Typeface encounters space encounters typeface" (Akzidenz-Grotesk) The typeface "Akzidenz-Grotesk" one of the non-serif linear-antiqua typefaces was the inspiration for famous typefaces such as Helvetica or Univers. But this typeface is not altogether unknown, for it has applications in many areas. For example in the 70's, they were found in the New York Subways. The "Akzidenz Grotesk" is known among font connoisseurs as a character font that can withstand many things. I wanted to get to the bottom of this assertion and bring the typeface into situations or applications where they could not be made out. With the use of a video-projector, characters from Akzidenz Grotesk would be projected onto buildings and items in the city, and then photographically fixed (photographed).

Criteria for the selection of individual buildings and characters will be defined for example, by size or dimensions so that the new image differs onto a DIN A4 sheet of paper from refractions and playful perspective effects that can be created with camera positions. Special attention was given to how the individual characters of the typeface withstood the environmental factors enforced upon it. The resulting images open up an alterreality presentation for the viewer, and like the typeface name itself is "grotesque (grotesk)". This was a wonderful discovery through this typography experiment. The findings can be seen printed on Choromolux cards DIN A5 size with Lumbeck-bindings. The slogan "Typeface encounters space encounters typeface" is grotesque and at the same time also enticing.

chrift begegnet Raum begegnet Schrift (Akzidenz Grotesk)
Original Work - "projected type" / 2007
Design: Tobias Battenberg

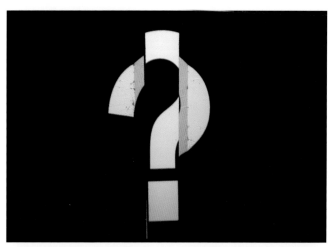 

「タイプフェース（フォント）と空間の遭遇」が彼の作品テーマである。「Akzidenz-Grotesk（サンセリフ書体のひとつ）」は、文字のストローク幅が一定な（linear-antiqua）セリフを持たない（「セリフ」＝ストロークの端の文字装飾部分）タイプフェースの代表例であり、Helvetica や Universe といった有名なタイプフェースの基にもなっているとされている。これらのタイプフェースは決して非一般的なものではなく、たとえば 70 年代のニューヨークの地下鉄などでは頻繁に使用された。Akzidenz-Grotesk は様々な用途に使用できるタイプフェースとしての絶対的な評価があるが、私は、これらの評価の基盤にまでもどり、このタイプフェースの文字として認知される限界を追求することを試みた。Akzidenz-Grotesk を使用した文字を、ビルや、街中の様々な風景に投影し、撮影をする。投影される文字やビルなどの組み合わせは、最終的に A4 サイズの写真として仕上がることを念頭におき、カメラポジションによって光のエフェクトがどう写真に影響するかを考慮し決めた。Akzidenz-Grotesk で表現される個々の文字が、どのように、そしてどの程度環境まで耐えることができ、その「文字性」を確立できるのかを観察した。実験の結果、これらの文字の投影は「別リアリティー」として見る者の目に映り、まさにその名の通り「グロテスク（奇怪さ）」を経験することがわかった。

Things I have learned in my life - 'Do It Without
Thinking Of Critics'
Original Work / 2008
Art Direction+Design: Julien Vallée & Karim
Zariffa

3 Dimensional Typography

The New York Times Magazine
– Motion branding
Stop Motion Animation /
The New York Times Magazine / 2008
Art Direction+Design+Animation: Julien Vallée

Softlightes, Heart Made of Sound
Music Video art direction / 2009
Design: Jonathan Zawada

You Only Live Once
Album Artwork / 2009
Design: Jonathan Zawada

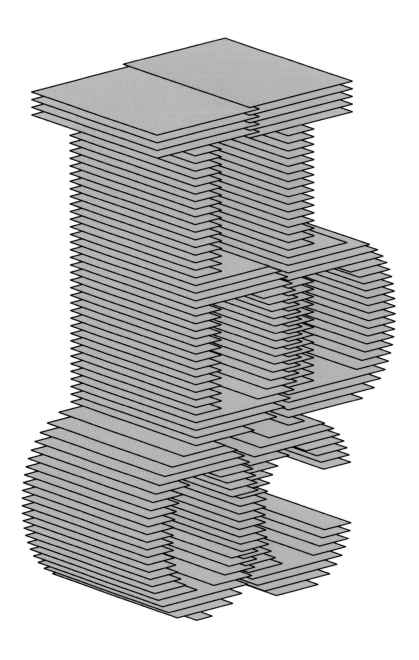

TDC Bccks/Twin Universe
Print Book, Web Book / Tokyo TDC / 2007
Design: 中村至男 Norio Nakamura

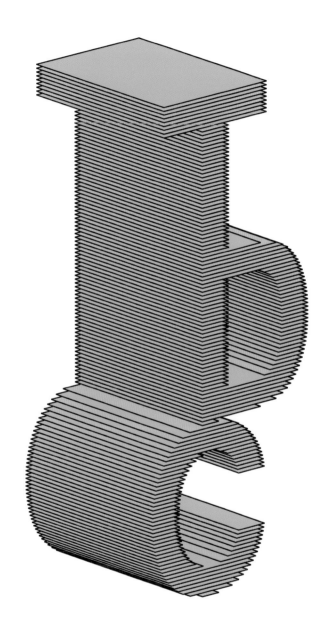

TDC Bocks/Twin Universe
Print Book, Web Book / Tokyo TDC / 2007
Design: 中村至男 Norio Nakamura

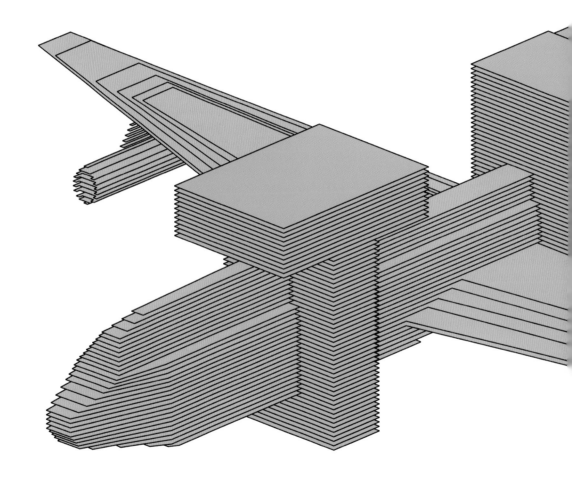

TDC Bccks/Twin Universe
Print Book, Web Book / Tokyo TDC / 2007
Design: 中村至男 Norio Nakamura

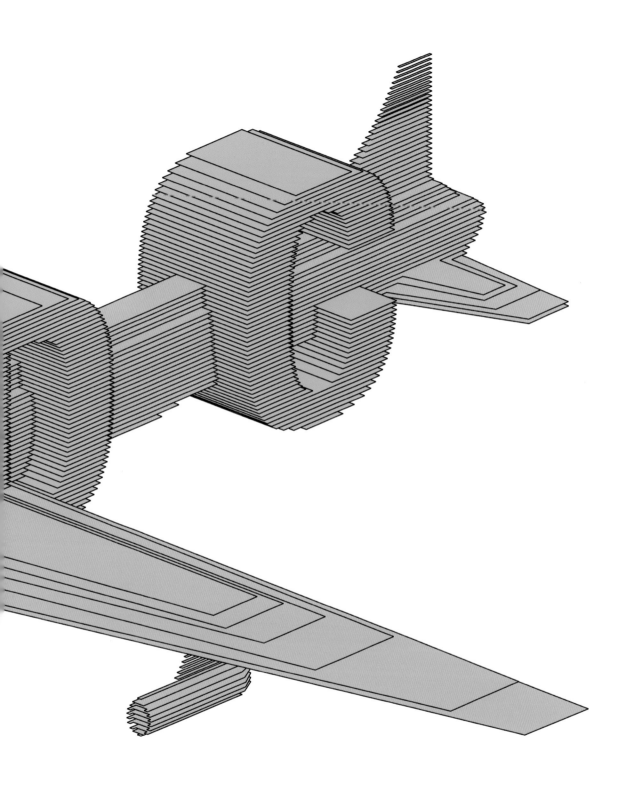

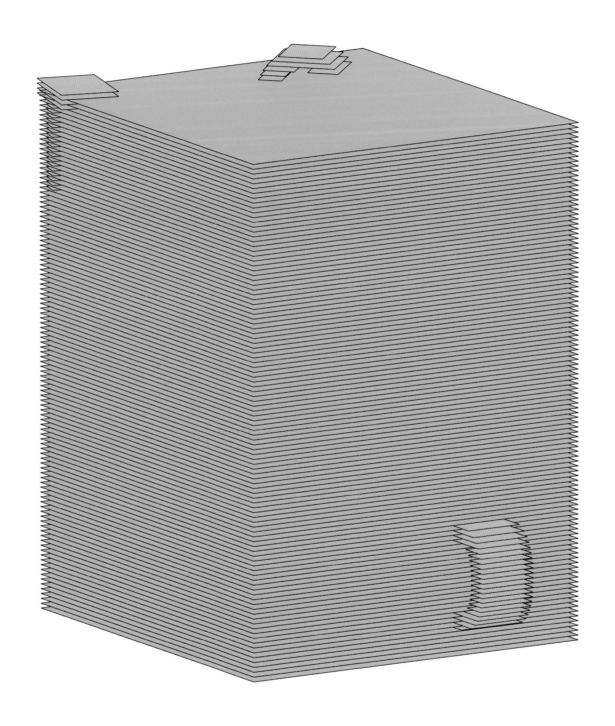

TDC Bccks/Twin Universe
Print Book, Web Book / Tokyo TDC / 2007
Design: 中村至男 Norio Nakamura

3 Dimensional Typography

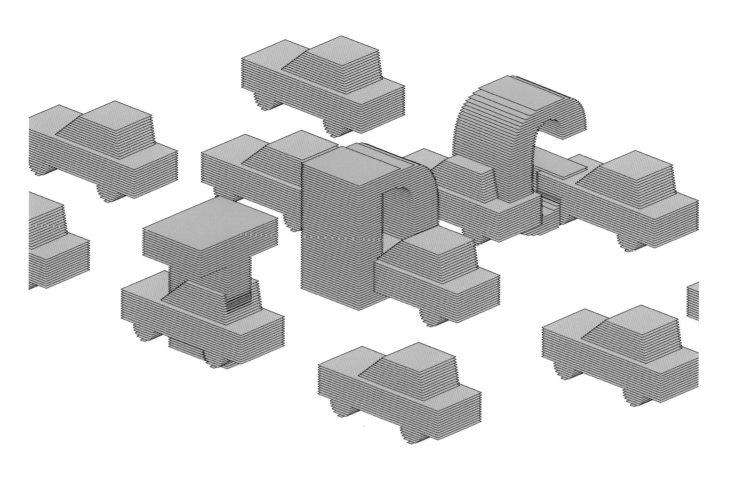

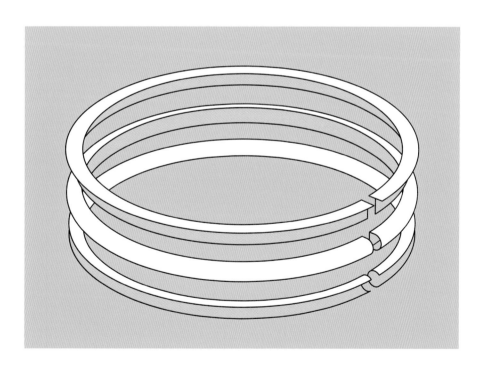

TDC Bccks/Twin Universe
Print Book, Web Book / Tokyo TDC / 2007
Design: 中村至男 Norio Nakamura

TDC Bccks/Twin Universe
Print Book, Web Book / Tokyo Tdc / 2007
Design: 中村至男 Norio Nakamura

〔 絵 と し て の 文 字 〕

読むという文字の機能を超えて、「絵」となってしまったタイポグラフィ。

メッセージを騙し絵のように伝えるタイポグラフィから、絵画として描かれたタイポグラフィまで。

絵として表現されたタイポグラフィの作品を紹介する。

Typography has risen above its original function of facilitating reading, to become 'pictures'.

We introduce works of typography that are created as pictorial images,

including some that convey messages through techniques akin to visual illusion, and others that take the form of painting.

2

typography
as pictures

CTP Template: VNL_12SP3
12 inch Album Sleeve (with 3mm spine)
Customer
Catalogue No. APOLLO109T
Job Title M.A.N.D.Y VS. BOOKA SHADE : BODY LANGUAGE

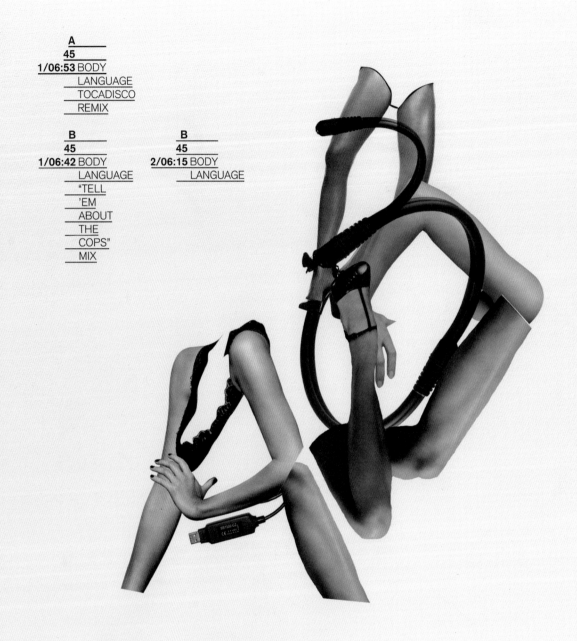

A
45
1/06:53 BODY
LANGUAGE
TOCADISCO
REMIX

B
45
1/06:42 BODY
LANGUAGE
"TELL
'EM
ABOUT
THE
COPS"
MIX

B
45
2/06:15 BODY
LANGUAGE

ALL TRACKS WRITTEN BY DJ PAT BO, PHIL D. YOUNG & BOOKA SHADE
PRODUCED BY M.A.N.D.Y. & BOOKA SHADE
PUBLISHED BY EDITION PERKY PARK & WARNER CHAPPELL
TRACK A1 REMIX & ADDITIONAL PRODUCTION BY TOCADISCO FOR WWW.TOCADISCO.COM
TRACK B1 REMIX & ADDITIONAL PRODUCTION BY ADAM WALTER
ENGINEERED BY FUNKAGENDA AT THE FUNK FARM, BIRMINGHAM
FOR AND ON BEHALF OF 24 MANAGEMENT / DEAN@24TWENTYFOUR.COM

DESIGNED WITH LOVE AT THE HORT / WWW.HORT.ORG.UK

(P) 2006 GET PHYSICAL MUSIC,
UNDER EXCLUSIVE LICENSE TO
UNIVERSAL-ISLAND RECORDS LTD.
APOLLO109T / LC 00407

0 602517 180475

M.A.N.D.Y. vs Booka Shade - Body Language
Record Cover / Get Physical Music / 2007
Design: HORT

M.A.N.D.Y.
VS.
BOOKA SHADE
BODY
LANGUAGE

booka shade   more!

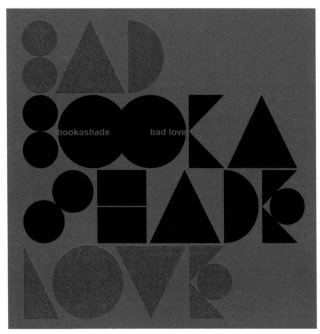

Booka Shade - More!
Album, Single Cover Artwork, Poster / Get
Physical Music / 2010
Design: HORT

Typography as Pictures

Galaxie 500
Screen Print Poster / Insound / 2009
Design: Mike Perry

6
Screen Print / YWFT / 2008
Design: Mike Perry

A-Z Landscape
Drawing / Personal Work / 2007
Design: Mike Perry

Typography as Pictures

We See Through things…
Drawing / Personal Work / 2007
Design: Mike Perry

Save Us
Drawing / Personal Work / 2007
Design: Mike Perry

Typography as Pictures

So Much Grows in Brooklyn
Drawing / Personal Work / 2006
Design: Mike Perry

Dwell Logotype
Drawing / Dwell Magazine / 2007
Design: Mike Perry

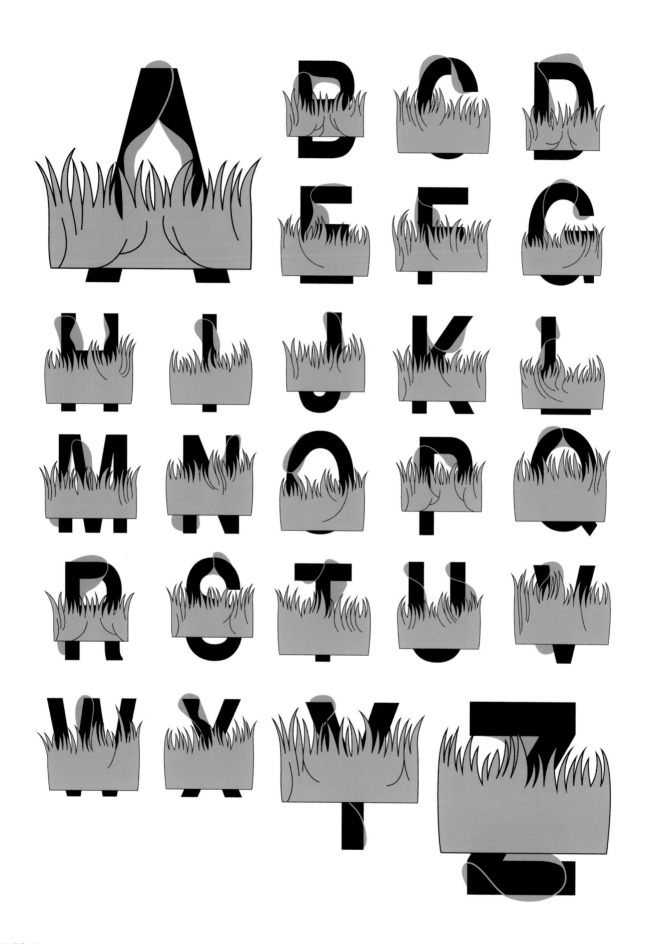

ABE #12 Typeface
Typeface / Non-commercial Work / 2005
Design: Kazuhide Abe

Typography as Pictures

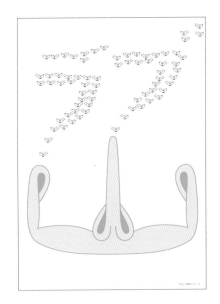

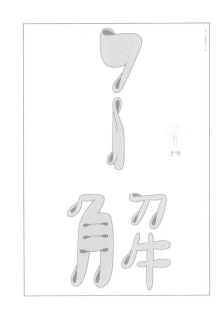

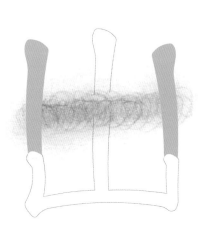

武蔵野美術大学 平成21年度
博士後期課程研究発表展
武蔵野美術大学2号館 1F／gFAL／FAL
10：00〜19：00（土曜日は17：00まで）

Hakushi
Koukikatei

博士

後期課程研究発表

展

Kenkyu
Happyo
Ten

《前期》2010年4月5日（月）〜10日（土）　　《後期》2010年4月12日（月）〜17日（土）

朴 令順 *Young-Soon Park* [gFAL]　　小池 浩央 *Hirohisa Koike* [gFAL]

野村 叔子 *Syukuko Nomura* [FAL]　　小松崎 晃 *Akira Komatsuzaki* [FAL]

うれしい気持ちシリーズ
Poster / Non-commercial Works / 2004
Design: Kazuhide Abe

金閣寺
造形文字 / Non-commercial Work / 2004
Design: Kazuhide Abe

仙人
造形文字 / Non-commercial Work / 2004
Design: Kazuhide Abe

武蔵野美術大学 博士後期課程研究発表展
ポスター
Poster / 武蔵野美術大学 / 2010
Design: Kazuhide Abe

Typography as Pictures

071

Canyons EP
12" vinyl Packaging / Hole In The Sky / 2008
Design: Jonathan Zawad

Typography as Pictures

Muscles - The Lake
12" vinyl / 2008
Design: Jonathan Zawada

Muscles - Sweaty
12" vinyl / 2008
Design: Jonathan Zawada

55DSL SS08 Collection
Promotional film, Business cards / 55DSL / 2008
Design: Bunch, Illustration: Omega! the Kid
Phoenix

Typography as Pictures

Work Hard Then Party Harder
Poster / 55DSL / 2008
Design: Bunch, Illustration: Omega! the Kid Phoenix

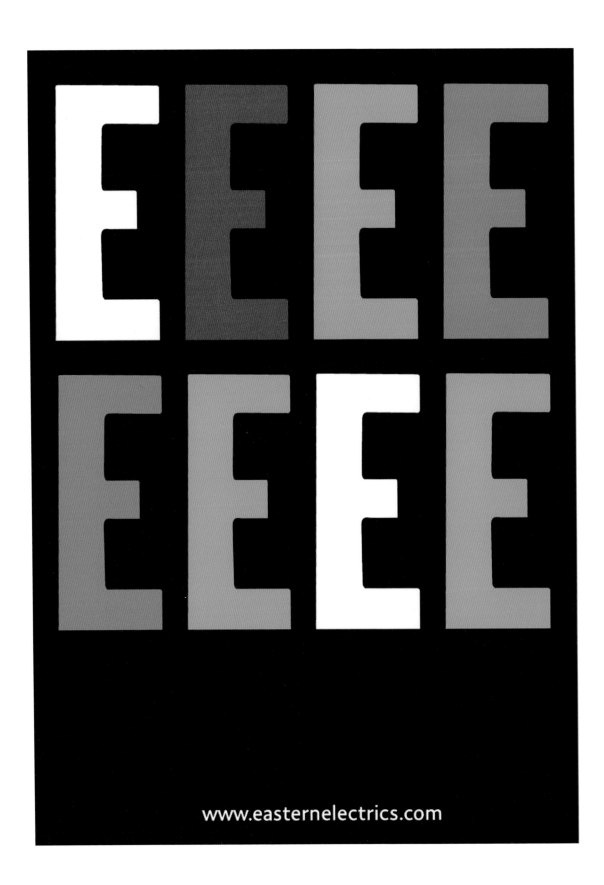

Poster / Eastern Electrics / 2010
Design: Bunch

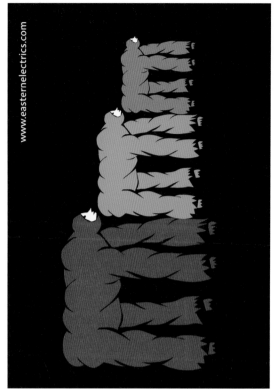

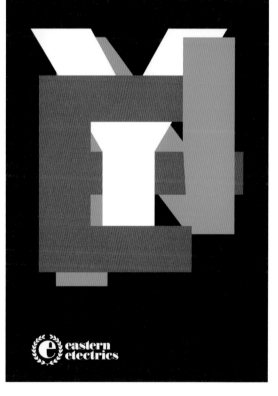

Poster & Flyer / Eastern Electrics / 2010
Design: Bunch, Illustration: Omega! the Kid
Phoenix

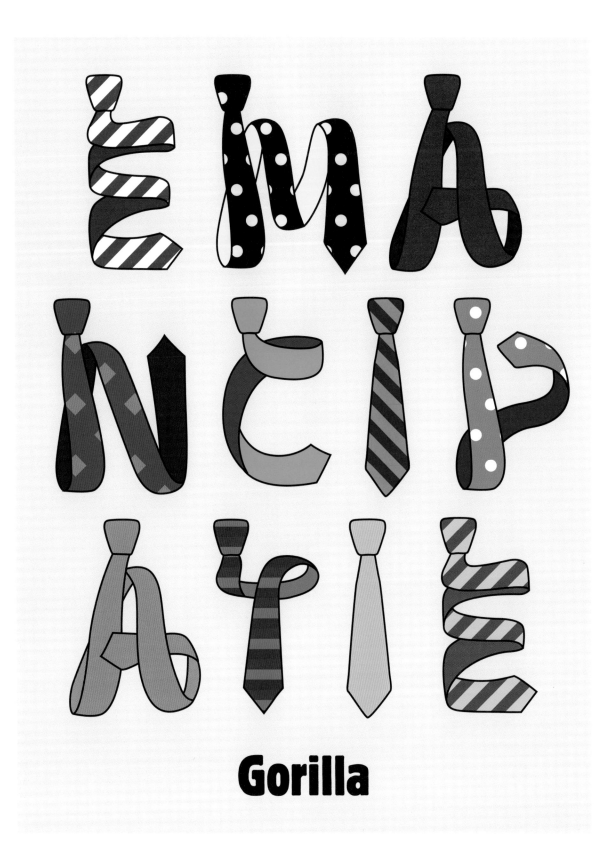

Gorilla

GORILLA
Visual column / De Volkskrant / 2006-2010
Design: Lesley Moore

Kit Out Your Studio
Illustration / Computer Arts UK / 2010
Illustration: István Szugyiczky

Gluttony
Illustration / XENO.WS / 2008
Illustration: István Szugyiczky

Typography as Pictures

Borderline
Illustration / XENO.WS / 2008
Illustration: István Szugyiczky

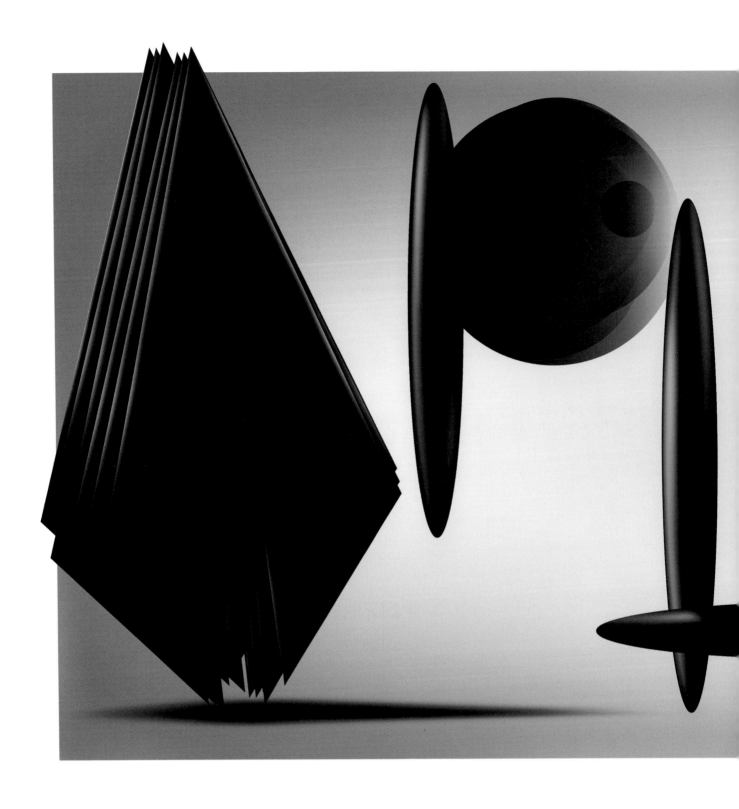

Aplomb
Illustration / Artistic Images / 2011
Illustration: István Szugyiczky

No Relation
Illustration / XENO.WS / 2009
Illustration: István Szugyiczky

Beautiful Decay
Illustration / Beautiful Decay / 2008
Illustration: István Szugyiczky

OLIMPÍADA
CRISIS
OBAMA

No Relation
Illustration / N/A / 2008
Illustration: István Szugyiczky

Typography as Pictures

Bipolar
Illustration / XENO.WS / 2009
Illustration: István Szugyiczky

Les Fleurs Du Mal
Sleeve / "A" is for acid / 2008
Illustration: István Szugyiczky

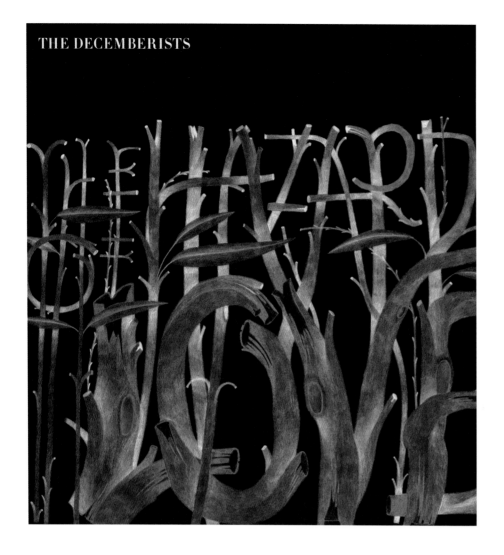

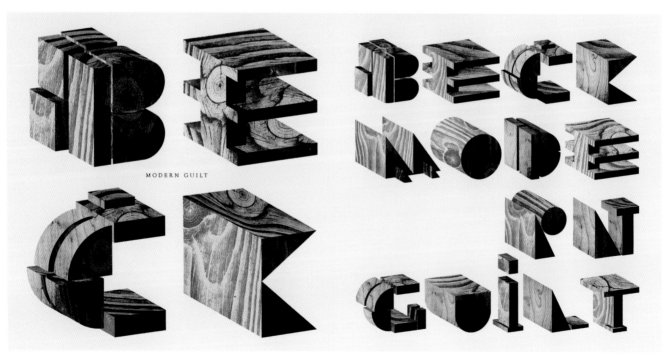

MODERN GUILT

The Decemberists - The Hazards of Love
Record Sleeve / Capitol Records / 2009
Design: Mario Hugo, Collaboration: Carson Ellis

Beck - Modern Guilt
Record Sleeve (Unused) / Interscope Records / 2008
Design: Mario Hugo

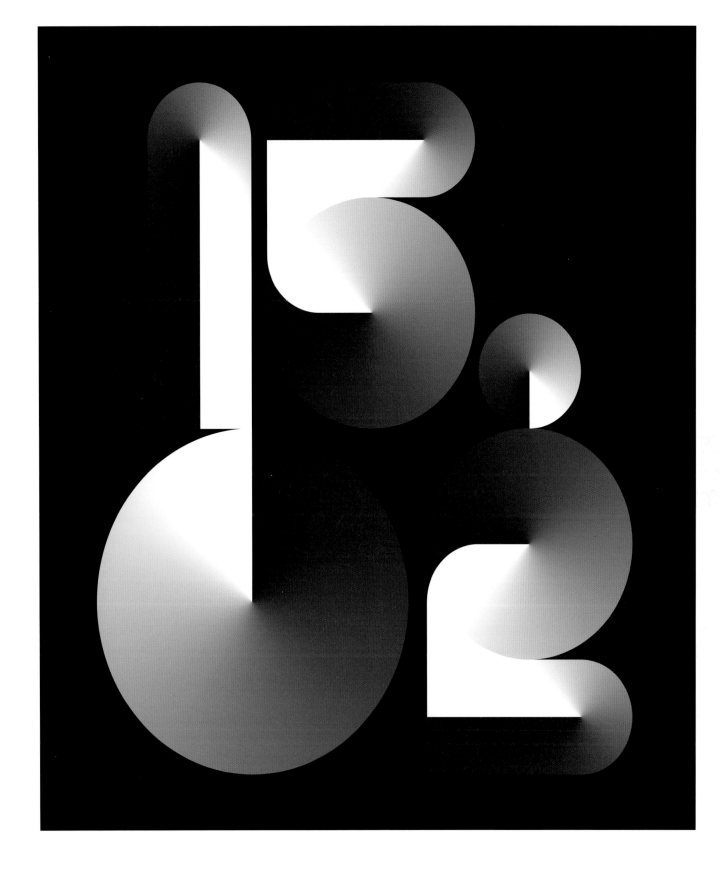

15.02
Editorial / Wired Magazine / 2006
Design: Mario Hugo

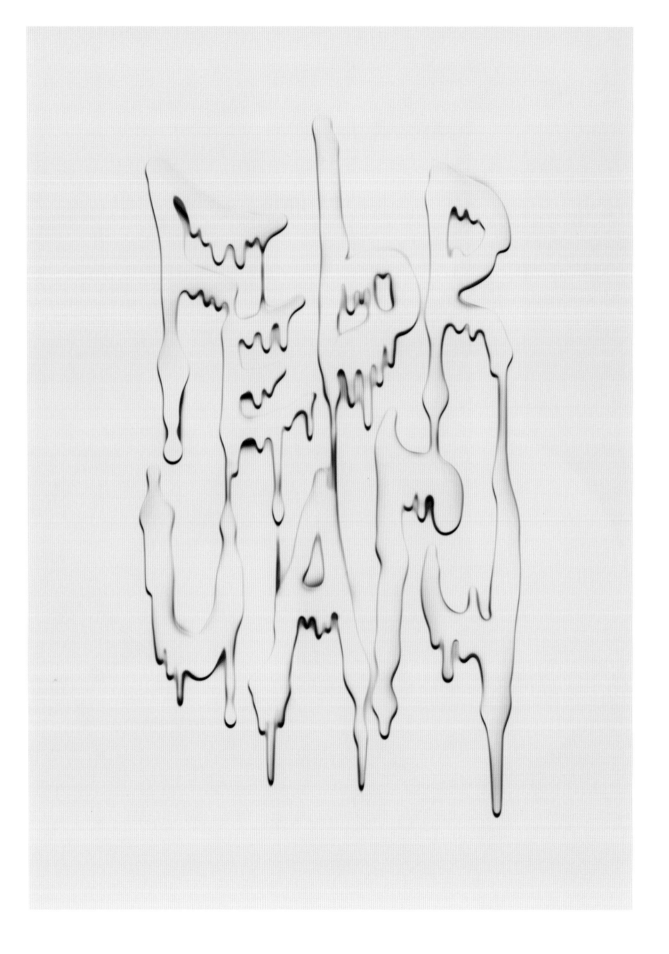

February
Calendar / LifeLounge / 2009
Design: Mario Hugo

Cos/Mes
Record Sleeve / ESP Institute / 2010
Design: Mario Hugo

Philopoemen
Record Sleeve / Daniel Ciardi / 2009
Design: Mario Hugo

Nowhere to Go, Everything to See
Personal Project / It's Nice That / 2007
Design: Mario Hugo

〔 構 成 の 遊 び 〕

言語表現から造形表現としてのタイポグラフィへ。

平面を構成する要素としての文字を用いて試みられた、グラフィカルな実験と実践。

その成果はタイポグラフィの未来を照らし続けてきた。自由自在に踊り、遊ぶような、タイポグラフィの表現を紹介する。

From linguistic to compositional expression.

A focus on letters as elements of planar composition, and the associated graphic-oriented experiments and practices

whose products have always shined light upon the future of typography.

We introduce typographical expressions that almost give the impression of free dancing and playing.

3

the composition of
typog**(R)**aphy

The Composition of Typography

In Other Words···
Selection of Printed Works / Self-Initiated, also
commissioned by Eastside Projects and Eye
Magazine / 2009
Design: OK-RM

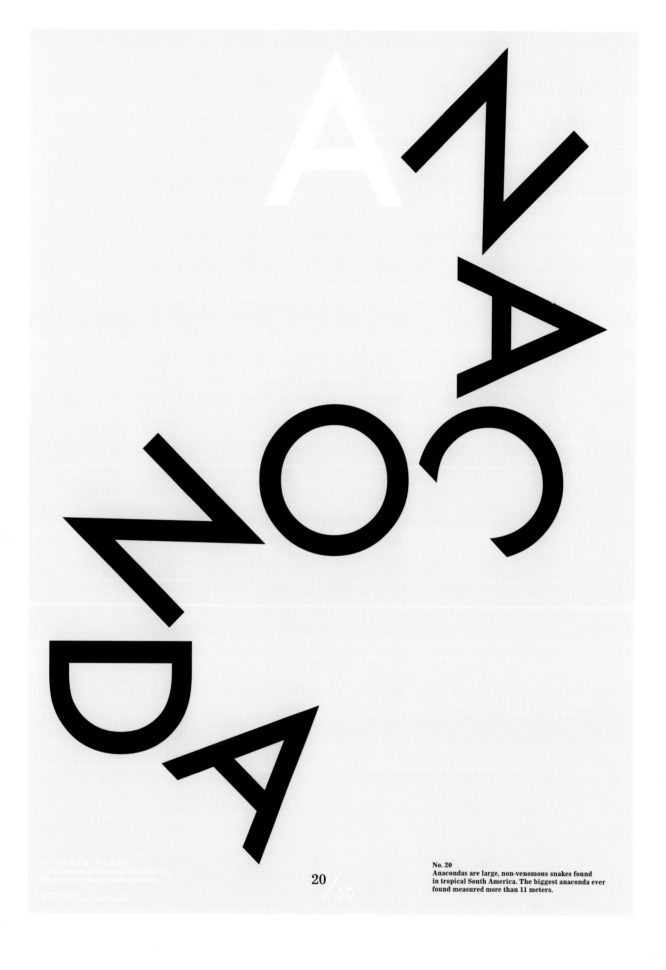

20 / 50

No. 20
Anacondas are large, non-venomous snakes found
in tropical South America. The biggest anaconda ever
found measured more than 11 meters.

097

FREEDOM FROM WANT
PART 2 OF 4

SEPTEMBER — OCTOBER
2010

Free
to
Air

(HEALTH, SANTÉ, SALUD, स्वास्थ्य, 健康)

Free to Air
Campaign / Film and Video Umbrella / 2009
Design: OK-RM

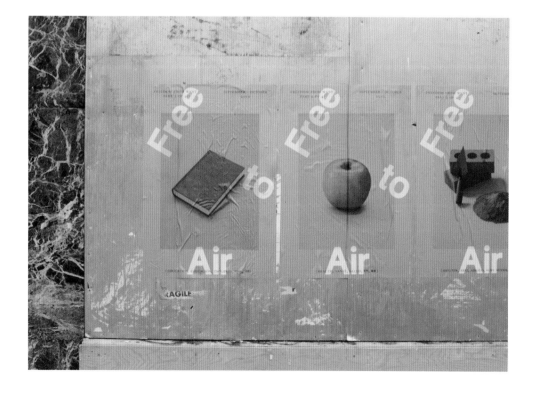

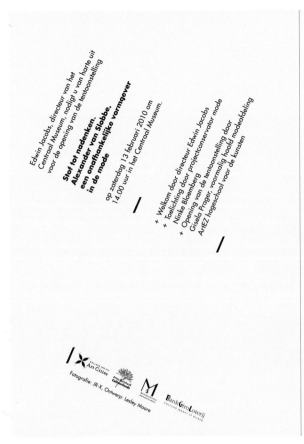

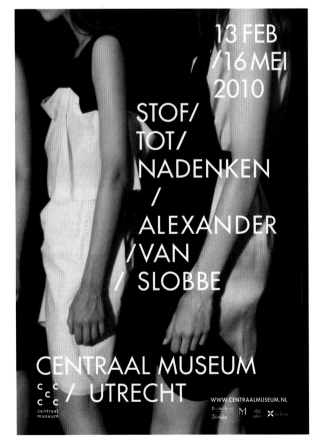

CENTRAAL MUSEUM / ALEXANDER VAN
SLOBBE
Poster Design and Invitation / ALEXANDER
VAN SLOBBE / 2010

Design: Lesley Moore, Photography: Joke
Robaard

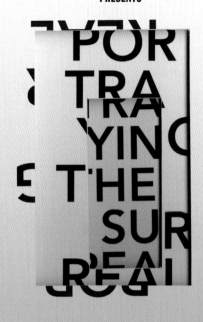

{ BLaTON & RYPSON }
aNTHROPOLOGiSTS iN aRT
PRESENTS

PORTRaYiNG THE SURREaL ~
THREE GENERaTiONS iN POLiSH PHOTOGRaPHY

WM GaLLERY & RODERS WiNEHaLL

{ BLaTON & RYPSON }
aNTHROPOLOGiSTS iN aRT
PRESENTS

iDENTiTY / UNTiTLED

CaTaRiNa aiMÉE DaHMS & MJ TURPiN
WM GaLLERY, NOVEMBER 13~20, 2010

{ BLaTON & RYPSON }
aNTHROPOLOGiSTS iN aRT
PRESENTS

Colour
Tales

aN aRTiSTIC RESEaRCH iNTO THE QUaLiTY OF COLOUR
BY LESLEY MOORE

MUSiC BY MaCHiNEFaBRiEK
STORYTELLING BY SaHaND SaHEBDiVaNi

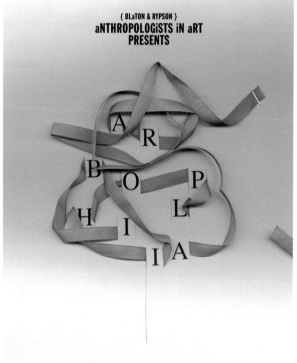

{ BLaTON & RYPSON }
aNTHROPOLOGiSTS iN aRT
PRESENTS

aRBOPHiLia ~ THE LOVE OF TREES
BY CECYLia MaLiK aND WaNDa MiCHaLaK
aT WM GaLLERY
MaY 14TH THROUGH JUNE 11TH 2011

ANTHROPOLOGISTS IN ART
Series of Invitations for Exhibitions /
ANTHROPOLOGISTS IN ART / 2010-2011
Design: Lesley Moore

Timid Tiger - Timid Tiger And The Electric Island
Columbia Records / CD artwork / 2010
Design: HORT

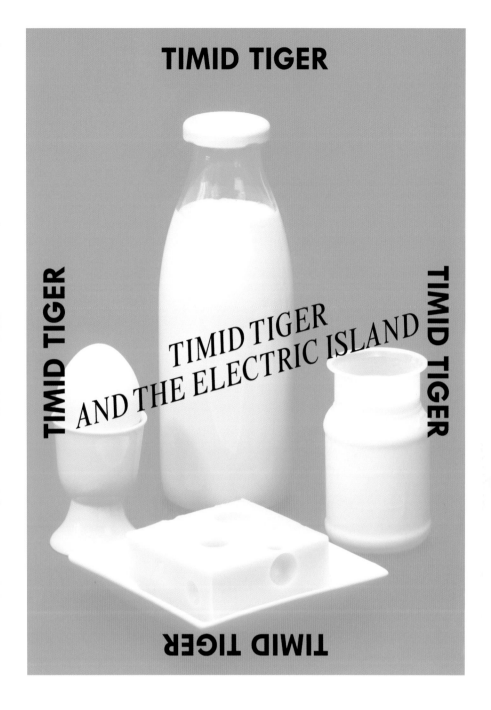

LEASE

D TIGER

AND
THE
ECTRIC
LAND

RELEASE

D TIGER
ECTRIC ISLAND

19
02
2010

RELEA

Timid Tiger - Timid Tiger And The Electric Island
Columbia Records / Promotional booklet / 2010
Design: HORT

TEMAConsult
Pencils / TEMAConsult / 2010
Design: HORT

TEMAConsult
Compliment Cards, Address Stickers /
TEMAConsult / 2010
Design: HORT

The Composition of Typography

TEMAConsult
Letterheads / TEMAConsult / 2010
Design: HORT

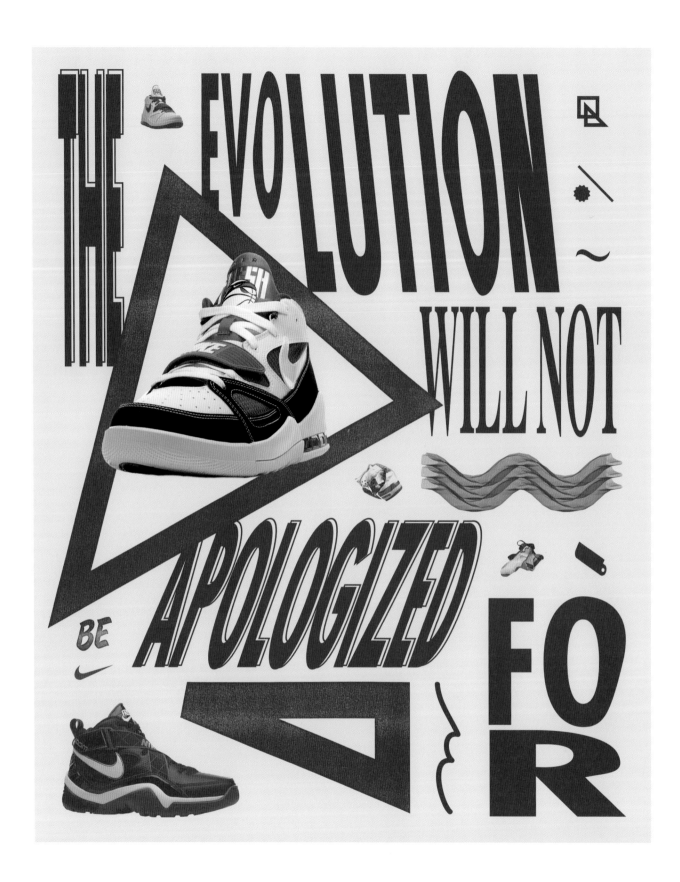

Nike Refresh Campaign
Posters, Banners, Murals / Nike / 2010
Design: HORT

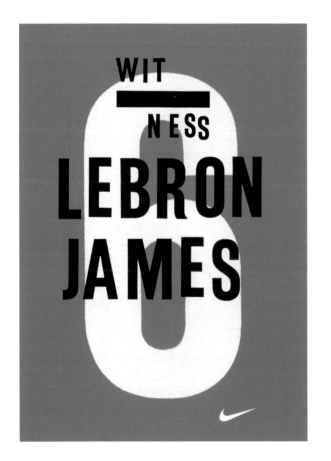
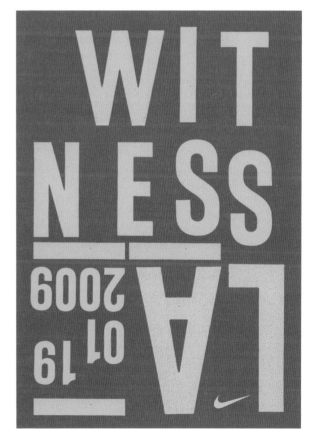

LeBron James Witness Campaign
Posters, Banners, Murals, Apparel, Promotional
Material etc. / Nike / 2009
Design: HORT

Le Théâtre Permanent
Visual identity for a theater event /
Tu Nantes / 2011
Design: Akatre

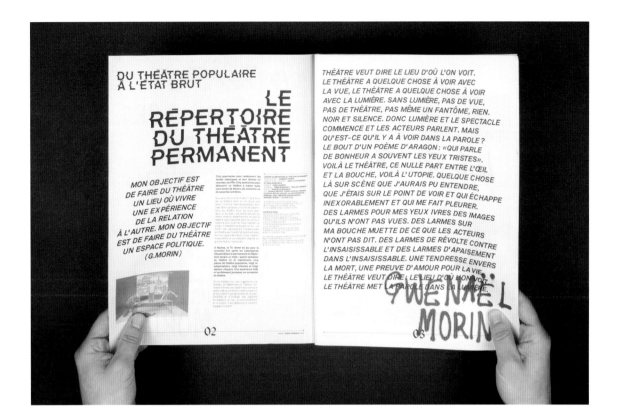

ACT
Poster campaign / Alexandra Bachzetsis & Lies
Vanborm / 2006

Design: Daniël Maarleveld, Collaboration: Lukas
Zimer, Julian Hagen

The Composition of Typography

ACT was a performance of Alexandra Bachzetsis & Lies Vanborm during the festival "If I can't dance" which took place in "de Appel", an art centre in Amsterdam. The purpose of the campaign was to create a buzz around the event and was part of 10 campaigns by Rietveld academy students. Our campaign divided all the information on separated posters. These posters where first placed separately giving them a different meaning/context. In a second run the missing information was added.

ACTは、アムステルダムのアートセンターである「ド・アペル」で開催された「If I Can Dance」の会期に、Alexandra Bachzetsis と Lies Vanborm により催されたパフォーマンスである。この催しの目的はイベントの目玉となるものを作ることで、リートベルト・アカデミーの学生による10個のキャンペーンのうちの一つだった。私たちのキャンペーンはすべての情報を別々に分けられたポスターに分断した。始めにこれらのポスターを別々に配置することにより、それらに違った意味合いやコンテクストを持たせた。二週目にはそこから欠けていた情報が加えられた。

MAN
VS
MACHINE

BLAAK HOMME

AUTUMN WINTER 2009

11H00 VENDREDI

23 JANVIER 2009

DOOR STUDIOS

9-9 BIS RUE

LESDIGUIÈRES 75004 PARIS

RSVP CRISTOFOLI PRESS

+33 (0) 1 44 84 49 49

INFO@CRISTOFOLIPRESS.FR

BLAAK
HOMME
SPRING
SUMMER
2009

Contact
Marcus Black
+44 (0) 7801 553 683

BLAAK - AW 09/10 Invite
Invitation / 2009
Design: Thorbjørn Ankerstjerne

BLAAK - Window Display
Window Display / 2009
Design: Thorbjørn Ankerstjerne

BLAAK - Boutique Inauguration
Invitation / 2009
Design: Thorbjørn Ankerstjerne

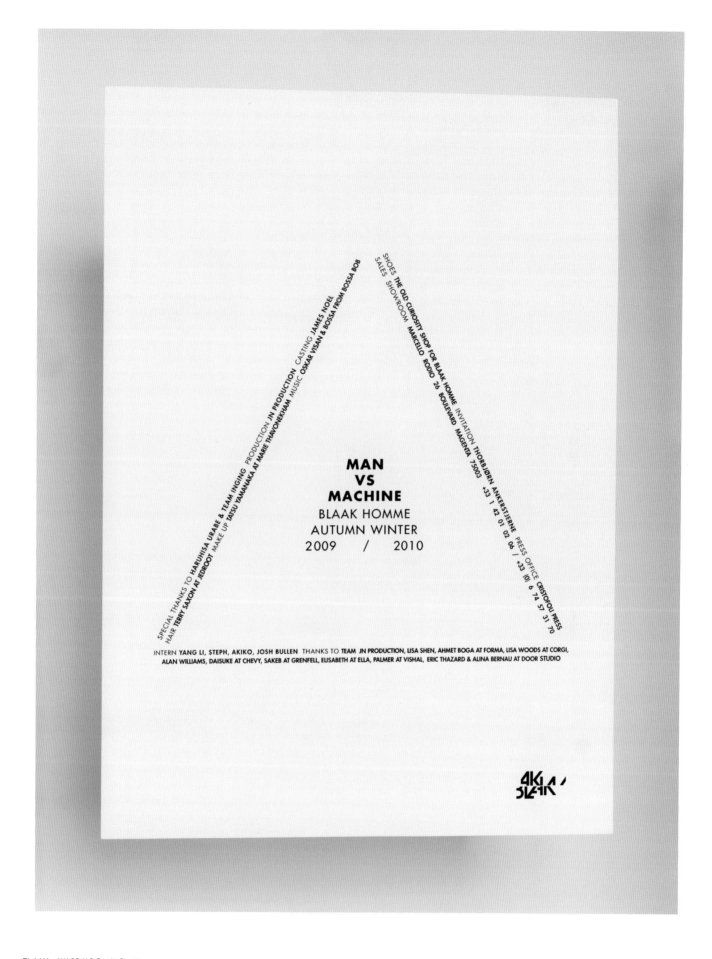

**MAN
VS
MACHINE**
BLAAK HOMME
AUTUMN WINTER
2009 / 2010

INTERN **YANG LI, STEPH, AKIKO, JOSH BULLEN** THANKS TO **TEAM JN PRODUCTION, LISA SHEN, AHMET BOGA AT FORMA, LISA WOODS AT CORGI,**
ALAN WILLIAMS, DAISUKE AT CHEVY, SAKEB AT GRENFELL, ELISABETH AT ELLA, PALMER AT VISHAL, ERIC THAZARD & ALINA BERNAU AT DOOR STUDIO

BLAAK - AW 09/10 Credit Sheet
Credit Sheet / 2009
Design: Thorbjørn Ankerstjerne

A Gentle Invasion - Auke de Vries
Poster / 2010
Design: Niessen & de vries

The Composition of Typography

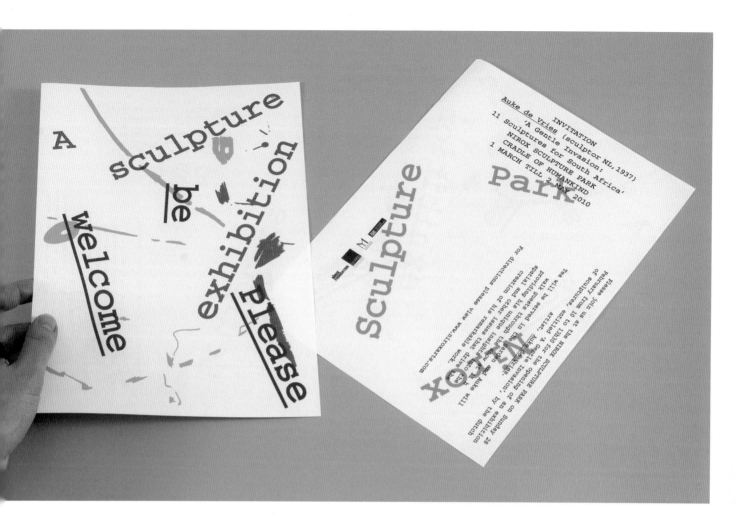

〔 視 覚 に よ る 効 果 〕

文字に施された様々なエフェクト。

文字を彩る視覚的な表現には、目眩のするようなオプアートの手法、プログラミングのパターン、アナログなエフェクトまで、現在には無数の手法がある。

視覚効果をグラフィックにまで昇華させている作品を紹介する。

Diverse effects can be embedded into letters.

Their visual qualities can be modulated through numerous methods, including dizzying Op Art techniques, programmed patterns, and analog effec

We introduce works that sublimate visual effects to the point of being full graphic designs in themselves.

4

the optical effects of typogr△phy

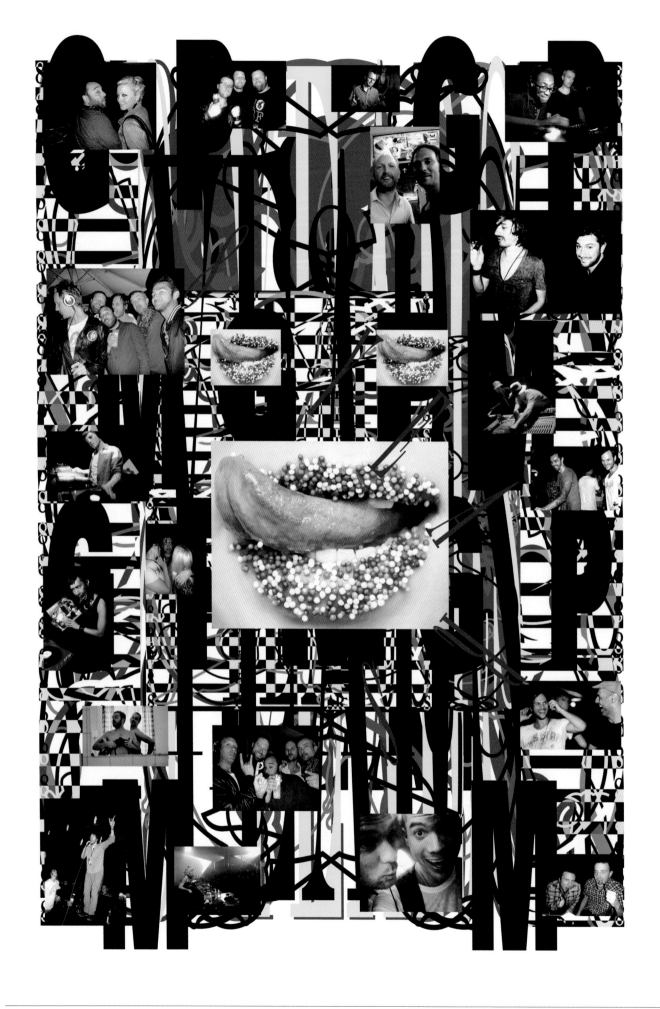

The Optical Effects of Typography

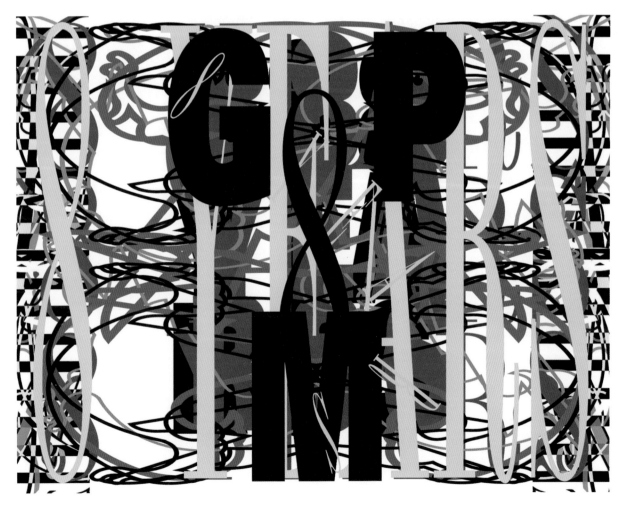

8 Years Of Get Physical Music
Poster / 2010
Design: HORT

8 Years Of Get Physical Music
CD artwork, record cover art work / 2010
Design: HORT

NOISE 05
Advertisement / YouWorkForThem / 2009
Design: Travis Stearns

The Optical Effects of Typography

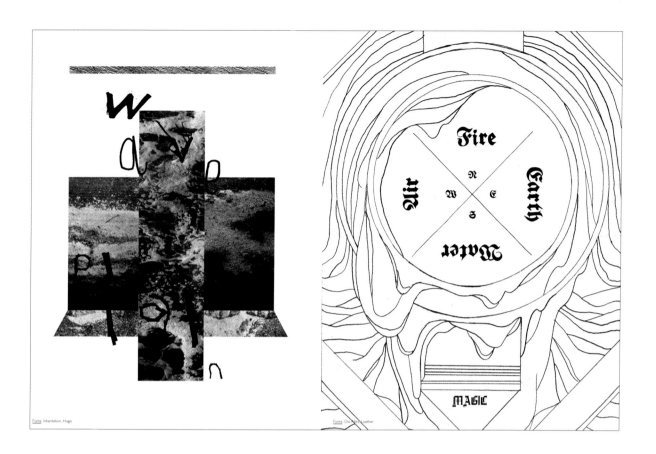

LOREM IPSUM VADE MECUM
Book Spread / YouWorkForThem / 2009
Design: Travis Stearns

Back Again
Experimental typography / Self / 2010
Design: Travis Stearns

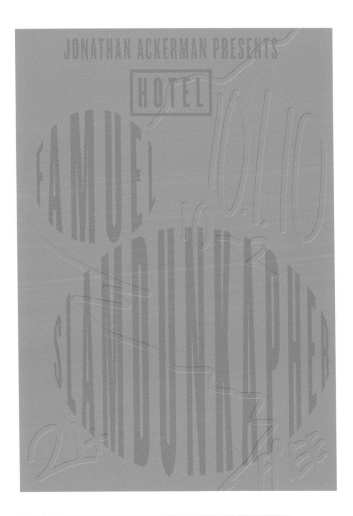

nick and eddie
1612 harmon place
minneapolis

djs

the moongoons
shannon blowtorch
wzz wnshp
plain ole bill

rsvp:
moongoons.com/bomp

HOTEL - October
Flyer / Jonathan Ackerman / 2010
Design: Travis Stearns

BOMP - No. 4 - January
Flyer / BOMP Minneapolis / 2011
Design: Travis Stearns

BOMP - October
Flyer / BOMP Minneapolis / 2010
Design: Travis Stearns

SUNDAY 9 26 2010

3$ with RSVP
5$ without

7:00   2:00

The Moongoons
PD Spinlove
DJs   Mike 2600
Plain Ole Bill
Famuel
Sovietpanda
The Stay Spun

NIGHT

DANCE PARTY

moongoons.com/rsvp

First Avenue | **All Ages until 9:45pm** | **18+ after 9:45pm**

Sunday Night Dance Party
Flyer / SNDP / 2010
Design: Travis Stearns

DJHAMANSUTRA.COM

N E W

Y O R K

love, dream & hip hop
Poster, Din A 1 / Hamansutra / 2011
Design: Tobias Röttger

MRI vs UES
Record Sleeve / Resopal / 2010
Design: Tobias Röttger

HAPPY MERRY NEW YEAR 8 HAPPY MERRY CHRISTMAS 8 HAPPY NEW YEAR FROM

from Hort

Happy Merry
Postcard / Hort / 2009
Design: Tobias Röttger

The PenJet project is a collaboration of Rietveld Academie students Jaan Evart, Julian Hagen and Daniël Maarleveld. The project has originated from the workshop "Uncommon Usage" given mond an adapted typeface for the PenJet emerged. Also adapted pictures were "printed" in several layers.

PenJetプロジェクトはリートベルト・アカデミーの生徒のジャン・エヴァート、ジュリアン・ハーゲン、そしてダニエル・マーレベルトによるコラボレーションである。このプロジェクトは「アンコモン・ユセージ」というワークショップに端を発するものであり、同ワークショップはPenJetの出現以来、採用されたタイプフェースにモンドを付け加えた。またここに採用された写真は数レイヤーにわたり「現像」されている。

PenJet
Poster series, magazine /
Personal Project / 2010

Design: Daniël Maarleveld,
Collaboration: Jaan Evart, Julian Hagen and
Daniël Maarleveld

Amsterdam, 28-June-2007
The exam committee of the Gerrit Rietveld
Academie hereby certifies that

Name
Dalin Aberfield

Born
09 April 1981

Place of birth
Amsterdam

Has successfully concluded the final exam of the graduate course
Design

In the field of
Graphic design

Examinee
Dalin Aberfield

Chairman of the committee
Samuel L. Baker

Secretary exam committee
Jolan Bencsik

Examiner(s)
Pauline Brisebois

The final exam consists of a written thesis and a public presentation.

Students who have passed their final exams of the Fine Arts Degree course may carry the title Bachelor of Fine arts (BFA); those who have finished the Design course may carry the title Bachelor of Design (BDes).

The Gerrit Rietveld Academie is an institution recognized by the Ministry of Education Culture and Science (Ministerie van OCW) for applied sciences. The Visual Arts and Design courses were last inspected in 2007.

Every tool has it's influence on how characters are formed. Think of: calligraphy or stencil-type. Digital tools, such as a filter, also have an influence on typography. That's how the diploma Akzidenz arose. An in between shape of the clear Akzidenz Grotesk and the excessive calligraphic visual interpretation of security paper and certificates. The loops generated by the tool react to the form of the character. This method has a total different impact on each size and variation of the character. This is how the official diplomas and communication around "Gra-Prijs" (Gerrit Rietveld Prize) have been designed. On the diploma the contra shape of this type has been used. This typographic layer was printed over with information by the administration office.

すべてのツールはキャラクターの形成に影響を及ぼす。例としては、カリグラフィー、ステンシルなど。フィルターのようなデジタルツールもタイポグラフィーに影響を与える。diploma Akzidenz が生まれたのはそのせいだ。明確な Akzidenz Grotesk の形と、賞状用紙の視覚的な過剰なカリグラフィ的な解釈の間の子である。この手法は、文字のあらゆるサイズやヴァリエーションに対してこれまでにないインパクトを持つものである。このようにして「グラ・プライズ」（ジェリット・リートベルト賞）の公式な免状とそれに関するコミュニケーションがデザインされた。その diploma にはこの書体の対極をなす形態が用いられている。このタイポグラフィ的なレイヤーは大学の管理局による情報とともに印刷された。

diploma & Gra price
Diploma / Rietveld Academie / 2007
Design: Daniël Maarleveld

sick helvetica
Research and Experiment / Original Work / 2006
Design: V&G

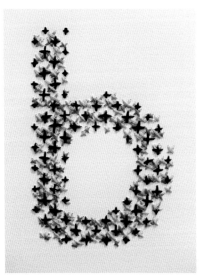

Experimental project exploring handmade print. Sans serif letterforms are stitched in four CMYK colours using exactly the same screen angles as in 4-colour printing process. Resulting colour is handmade "rich black", an equal blend of CMYK colours.

手製の印刷を追求する実験的なプロジェクト。四色印刷とまったく同じスクリーンの角度 を利用した四つの CMYK カラーでサンズ・セリフの字体が刺繍されている。結果としてそこに発色するのは手製の「リッチ・ブラック」であり、CMYK のブレンドと同じだ。

Printed Matter. Type
Hand embroidery on paper / 2008
Design: Evelin Kasikov

CMYK letters
Hand embroidery on Fabriano 5 Cold Pressed
White 300 gsm / 2011
Design: Evelin Kasikov

Pixellated lowercase letter-form 'a' is stitched using primary colours Cyan, Magenta and Yellow. The poster aims to bring together craft (cross-stitch) and technology (pixels and grids).

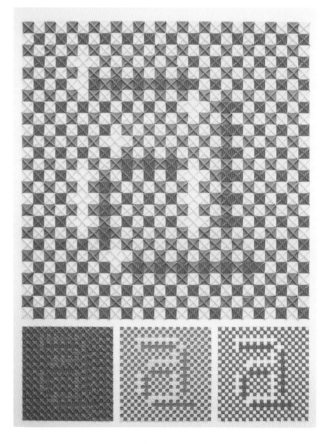

Simplify, simplify
Hand embroidery on Pergamenata White 110 gsm / 2008
Design: Evelin Kasikov

Gill Sans 'a'
Hand embroidery on Soft Cotton / 2008
Design: Evelin Kasikov

ピクセル化された小文字のaは シアン、マゼンダ、イエローという原色で刺繍されている。このポスターの狙いは、手工芸（クロスステッチ）とテクノロジー（ピクセル とグリッド）の融合である。

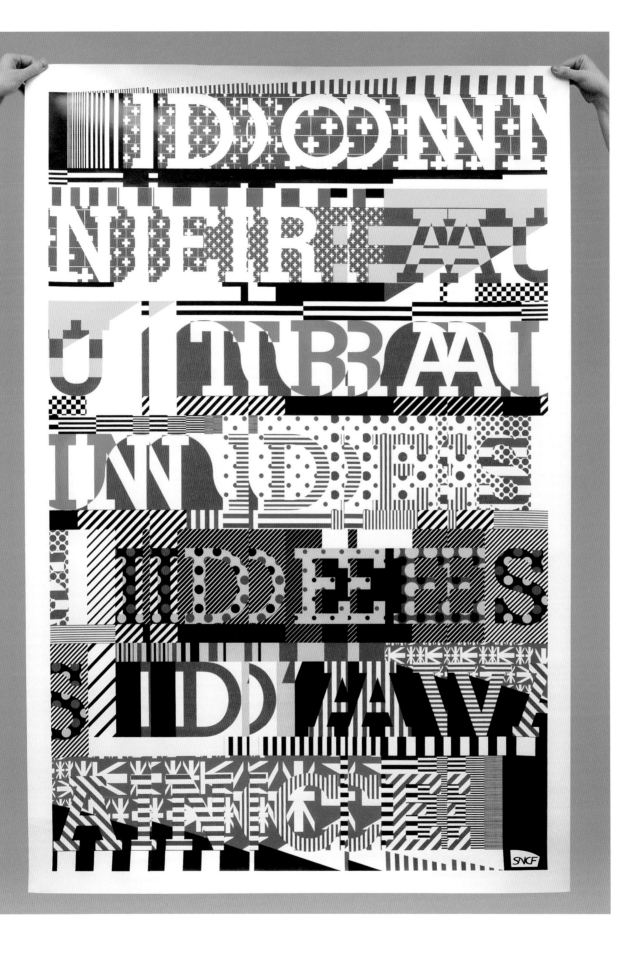

SNCF
Poster / 2008
Design: Niessen & de vries

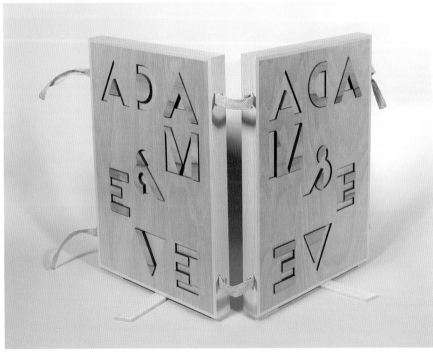

Special Box Adam & Eve
BOX / 2010
Design: Niessen & de vries

Adam & Eve
Poster / 2010
Design: Niessen & de vries

〔 手 描 き の 文 字 〕

様々な手法が混在するタイポグラフィの中でも、手描きタイポグラフィは、今また大きな潮流をなしている。

そこにはあらゆる画材、素材を用いて、自在に描かれた文字表現が生まれ続けている。

手描きタイポグラフィの現在進行形を紹介する。

Within the diverse options of typographic methods, hand-drawn typography is once again becoming a prominent trend.

Many different tools and materials are used in order to produce highly unique designs.

We introduce the state-of-the-art of hand-drawn typography.

5

hand-drawn

typograPhy

Flora
Illustration / Personal Project / 2010
Design: Sasha Prood

Coming This Summer
Illustration / Personal Project / 2011
Design: Sasha Prood

Dream Big
Poster / The Say Something Poster Project / 2011
Design: Sasha Prood

zieki
Apparel Graphic /
Scholz & Friends Warsaw / 2011
Design: Sasha Prood

Girls & Boys
Illustrations / crewcuts / 2010
Design: Sasha Prood

the FIRST EDITION
—— of ——
MY HAND DRAWN
FIELD STUDY INSPIRED
ALPHABET SETS

ILLUSTRATED
and DESIGNED
by SASHA PROOD

SASHAPROOD.COM

Botanica Caps
Poster / Personal Project / 2010
Design: Sasha Prood

Typoles
Original Work / 2009
Design: 大原大次郎 Daijiro Ohara

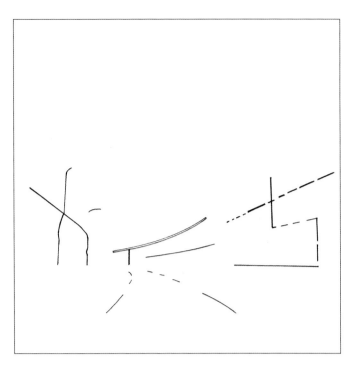

文字採集
Original Work / 2009
Design: 大原大次郎 Daijiro Ohara

SAKEROCK - MUDA
CD Jacket / Kakubarhythm / 2010
Design: 大原大次郎 Daijiro Ohara

MaNHATTAN - Giant Stomp
CD Jacket / Galactic / 2011
Design: 大原大次郎 Daijiro Ohara

星野源 - ばかのうた / CD Jackct /
SPEEDSTAR RECORDS / 2010
Design: 大原大次郎 Daijiro Ohara

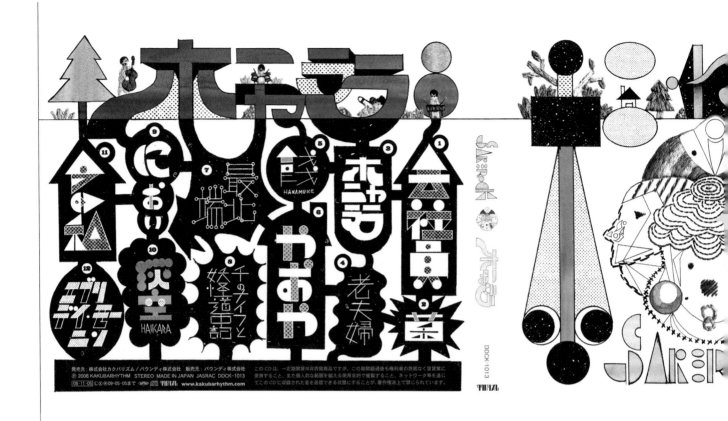

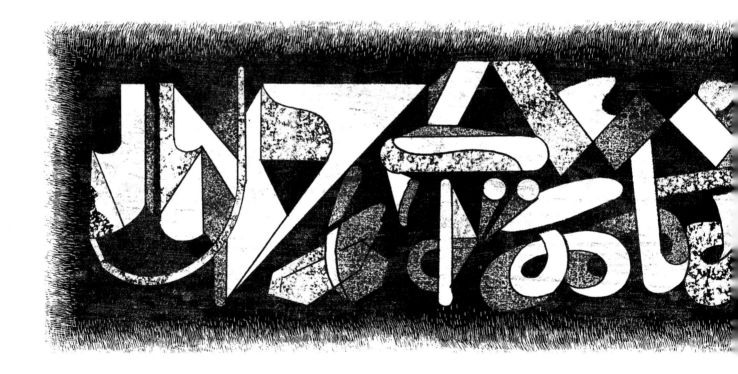

SAKEROCK - ホニャララ / CD Jacket /
Kakubarhythm / 2008
Design: 大原大次郎 Daijiro Ohara

HIFANA feat. 鎮座 DOPENESS - WAKE UP
Graphic for MV / W + K Tokyo Lab / 2010
Design: 大原大次郎 Daijiro Ohara

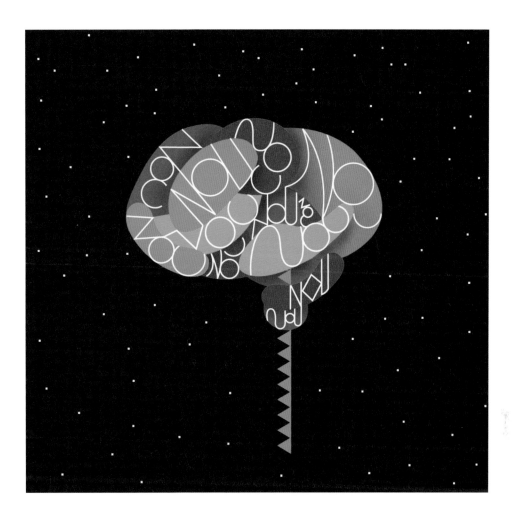

脳 - Sweet Memories
CD Jacket / Pan Pacific Playa / 2009
Design: 大原大次郎 Daijiro Ohara

裏フィック
T-shirts / ANSWR / 2010
Design: 大原大次郎 Daijiro Ohara

Hand-drawn Typography

SAKEROCK Back Drop
Back Drop for Live / Kakubarhythm / 2009
Design: 大原大次郎 Daijiro Ohara

There Is No Finish Line
T-shirts / NIKE / 2010
Design: 大原大次郎 Daijiro Ohara

Misc Type Mixed Media
Drawings / 2005-2009
Design: Mike Perry

Vibe magazine 10 most influintial songs
Drawings / Vibe Magazine / 2009
Design: Mike Perry

Free, Dumb
Cover Designs for a Notebook / 2010
Design: Jonathan Zawada

Hand-drawn Typography

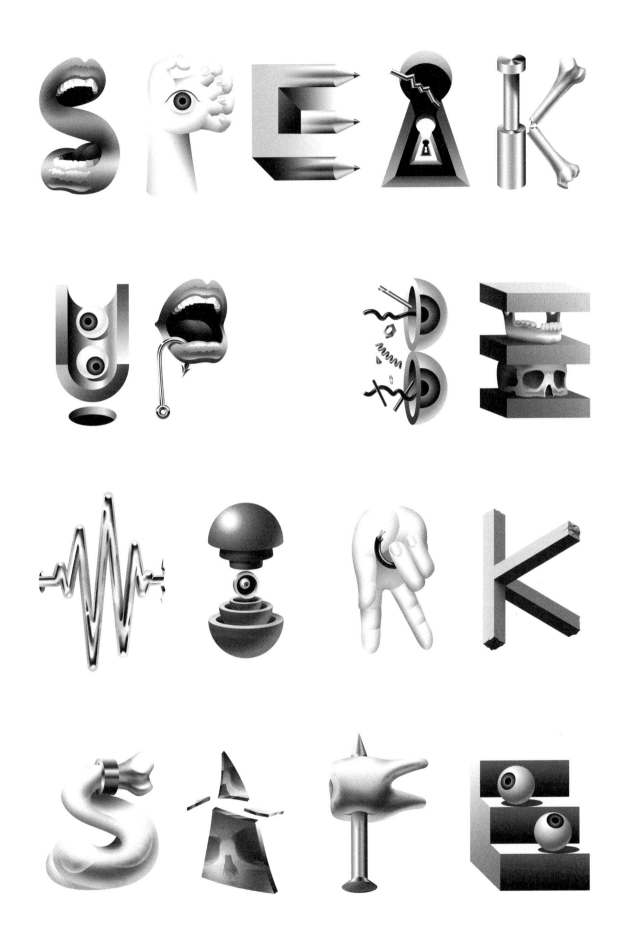

Bigmouth
Zine, Street Posters / 2009
Design: Jonathan Zawada

Glory Holes
Postcards, Exhibition Signage / 2009
Design: Jonathan Zawada

20MF Mythology
T-shirt Print Design / 2008
Design: Jonathan Zawada

MC
Logo Mark / 2010
Design: Jonathan Zawada

20MF Drapery
T-shirt Print Design / 2009
Design: Jonathan Zawada

L.O.T.
In Store Artwork / 2010
Design: Jonathan Zawada

Life in the Alphabet
Personal project / 2009
Design: Eika

Life is a magic
Personal project / 2010
Design: Eika

Vocabulary size
Sunday New York Times. / 2010
Design: Eika

Imagine
Lyric Culture / 2010
Design: Eika

Transitionists Titles
Illustrated type commission for Theme Magazine / 2010
Design: Deanne Cheuk

APRIL
Illustrated Type Commission / Fast Company
Magazine / 2010
Design: Deanne Cheuk

Always
Charcoal on Paper / 2009
Design: Deanne Cheuk

〔 ロ ゴ タ イ プ 〕

文字を主体にしたロゴデザインは、タイポグラフィというカテゴリーにおいて重要な仕事のひとつとなっている。
この章ではタイポグラフィの観点から、企業ロゴから実験的に作られたロゴまで、創意工夫に富んだロゴのデザインを紹介する。

Letter-based logo designs are one of the important sub-categories of typography as a whole.

In this section, we introduce everything from standard corporate logos to more experimental work, within the framework of typography.

6

typograp**HH**y
and logo design

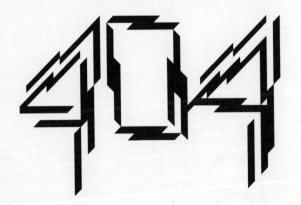

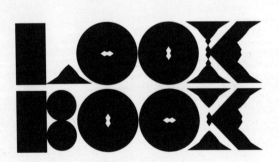

Error404
Logo Concepts / Error404 / 2008
Design: Travis Stearns

Error404
Logo Concepts / Error404 / 2008
Design: Travis Stearns

Ghost Of A Rose
Title / Self Commissioned / 2008
Design: Travis Stearns

Look Book
Logotype / Look Book / 2008
Design: Travis Stearns

Nico Vega
Logo Concept / Nico Vega Music / 2008
Design: Travis Stearns

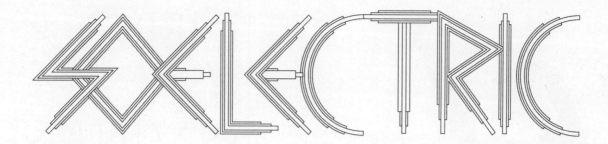

So Electric
Logo / The Moon Goons / 2008
Design: Travis Stearns

The Igloo
Logotype for blog / Self Commissioned / 2008
Design: Travis Stearns

Fenrir & Reynard
Logotype / Fenrir & Reynard Clothiers / 2008
Design: Travis Stearns

Wow Wow Wow
Logotype for blog / Self Commissioned / 2007
Design: Travis Stearns

I AM SOUND
Corporate Logotype / IAMSOUND Records /
2007
Design: Travis Stearns

FIG
T-shirt Print, Logo / INTERVIEW / 2010
Design: Mina Tabei

summer camp
Exhibition Logo / 2009
Design: Mina Tabei

LIBRO de KVINA
Publishing Level Logo / 2010
Design: Mina Tabei

LIBRO por MIELO
Art Project Logo / 2009
Design: Mina Tabei

Tento
Event Logo / SHIBUYA PARCO / 2010
Design: Mina Tabei

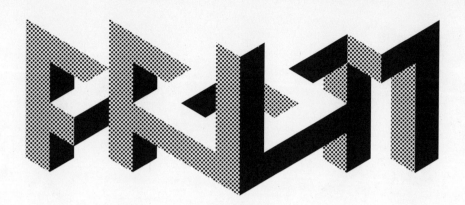

Salvation
T-shirt print, zine graphic / 2010
Design: Jonathan Zawada

Prism
Logo / 2009
Design: Jonathan Zawada

Parallel Management
Logo / 2010
Design: Jonathan Zawada

Tom Ugly
Logo / 2009
Design: Jonathan Zawada

Don't Forget to Smile
Logo / 2010
Design: Jonathan Zawada

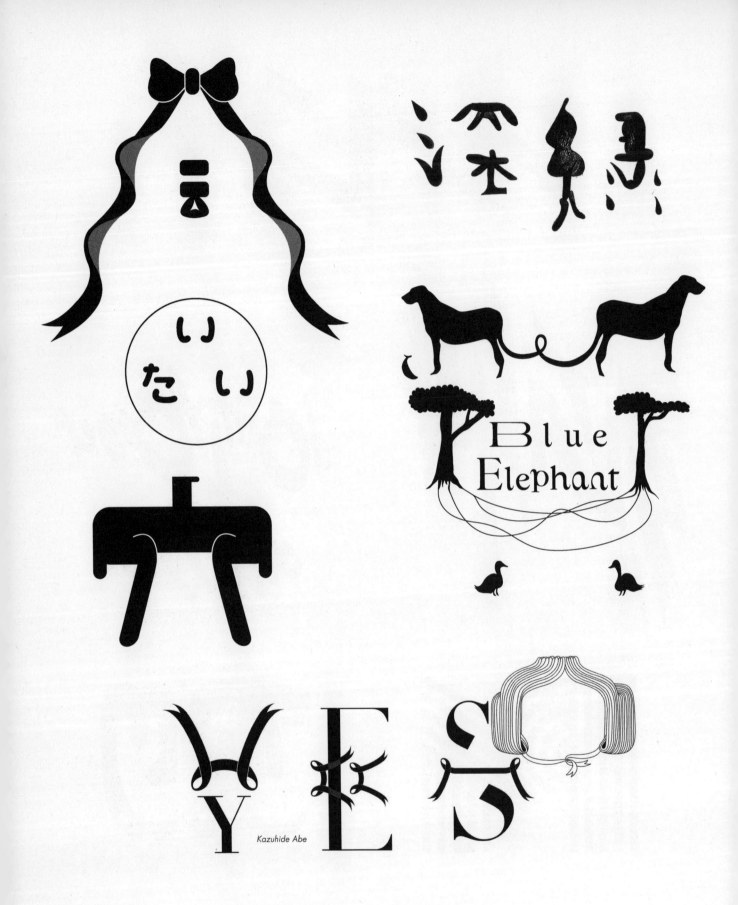

Kazuhide Abe

会いたい
造形文字 / Original Work / 2004
Design: 阿部一秀 Kazuhide Abe

深緑
造形文字 / Original Work / 2004
Design: 阿部一秀 Kazuhide Abe

穴
造形文字 / Original Work / 2004
Design: 阿部一秀 Kazuhide Abe

Blue Elephant
Logotype / Blue Elephant / 2007
Design: 阿部一秀 Kazuhide Abe

YES -SI O NO-
Logotype / siono / 2010
Design: 阿部一秀 Kazuhide Abe

Good

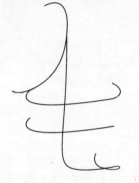

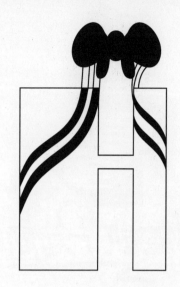

Roll

Good
造形文字 / Original Work / 2004
Design: 阿部一秀 Kazuhide Abe

毛糸
造形文字 / Original Work / 2004
Design: 阿部一秀 Kazuhide Abe

食うかい？
造形文字 / Original Work / 2004
Design: 阿部一秀 Kazuhide Abe

BLUE
造形文字 / Original Work / 2004
Design: 阿部一秀 Kazuhide Abe

H
造形文字 / Original Work /2004
Design: 阿部一秀 Kazuhide Abe

ニコニコ
造形文字 / Original Work / 2004
Design: 阿部一秀 Kazuhide Abe

ロール
造形文字 / Original Work / 2004
Design: 阿部一秀 Kazuhide Abe

AmourPropre
Illustration / Original Work / 2010
Design: Edrem

ISEEYOU
Illustration / Original Work / 2010
Design: Edrem

Goal
Illustration / Original Work / 2010
Design: Edrem

Clever
Illustration / Original Work / 2010
Design: Edrem

Shaper
Illustration / Original Work / 2010
Design: Edrem

PartTime
Illustration / Original Work / 2010
Design: Edrem

Lost Childwood
Illustration / Original Work / 2010
Design: Edrem

Mad
Illustration / Original Work / 2010
Design: Edrem

Grave
Illustration / Original Work / 2010
Design: Edrem

Hopeless
Illustration / Original Work / 2010
Design: Edrem

FeuCul
Illustration / Original Work / 2010
Design: Edrem

Gong
Illustration / Original Work / 2010
Design: Edrem

suck
Illustration / Original Work / 2010
Design: Edrem

Biography

Akatre
アキャト
http://www.ankerstjerne.co.uk/

Akatre was founded by Valentin Abad, Julien Dhivert and Sebastien Riveron. Akatre is a graphic design studio based in Paris (France) which works in visual identities, edition, photography, spaces on all medias. Akatre works mainly for cultural and luxury projects (CNAP, Galerie des Galeries (Lafayette' galleries), the theater TU Nantes, Issey Miyake, Kenzo... Akatre collaborates with galleries, choreographers and artists like Cindy Van Acker, Perrine Valli, Seulgi Lee, and creates for all its projects typographies and visuals (photo). It's an essential process to create and offer a personal point of view about a project.

パリを拠点にするグラフィックデザインスタジオ。Valentin Abad、Julien Dhivert、Sebastien Riveron によって設立し、ヴィジュアルアイデンティティ、出版物、写真、空間デザインを手がけている。Akatre は、主にカルチャーおよびラグジュアリー関連のプロジェクトに携わり、CNAP、Galerie des Galeries (Lafayette' galleries)、the theater TU Nantes、Issey Miyake、Kenzo などをクライアントとしている。また、ギャラリー、Cindy Van Acker、Perrine Valli、Seulgi Lee などの振り付け師やアーティストとコラボレーションをしており、それらのタイポグラフィ、ヴィジュアル（写真）を手がけている。それぞれのプロジェクトに対して、ユニークな視点を創造し、提案することが不可欠なプロセスだと考えている。

Bunch
バンチ
http://www.bunchdesign.com/

Bunch is a collective bound together by a collaborative and creative spirit. Our disciplines and clients are as diverse as we are and this is reflected in the broad range of work we cover, including, identity, literature, editorial, digital and motion. We love what we do. Established in 2002 with an international reach, from London and Zagreb, Bunch has an in-house team of specialists to deliver intelligent and innovative cross-platform solutions of communication design. Over the years we have been commissioned by many leading brands, companies and

the artistic industries, to build an impressive client base, such as, BBC, Nike, Red Bull, V&A, Diesel, 55 DSL, Sony, Sky, Mtv, HSBC...

協同的でクリエイティブなスピリットで繋がる集団。多様な専門分野において、様々なクライアントを持ち、アイデンティティ、文学、エディトリアル、デジタル、映像など幅広い領域の仕事を手がける。ロンドンとクロアチアのゼグロブを拠点に、2002年に設立。複数のプラットフォームに対応した知的で、革新的なコミュニケーションデザインのソリューションを導くため、インハウスの専門家チームを持っている。一流ブランド、企業、芸術関係の事業と共に数年に及ぶプロジェクトを手がけ、素晴らしいクライアントベースを築いている。主なクライアントに、BBC、Nike、Red Bull、V&A、Diesel 55 DSL、Sony、Sky、MTV、HSBC などがある。

Byggstudio
ビュックスタジオ
http://www.byggstudio.com/

Byggstudio is graphic designers Hanna Nilsson and Sofia Østerhus based in Stockholm, Sweden and Oslo, Norway. Byggstudio's graphic and interior design often follow their favourite interests; people, nature, food and history. Interest usually leads them to the Stockholm library at the start of a project - hours and 15 kg of books later texts and images are processed and transformed into design coloured by curiosity and layers of stories. Byggstudio often initiates their own projects, for example they collect second-hand plants, trees and their background stories in Vintage Plant. Hanna and Sofia both hold an MFA in Visual Communication from Danmarks Designskole (Copenhagen) in 2006.

ストックホルムとオスロを拠点に活動する、Hanna Nilsson と Sofia Østerhus によるデザインチーム。Byggstudio のグラフィックデザインやインテリアデザインは、二人のお気に入りのもの（人、自然、食べ物、歴史）をモチーフにしている。プロジェクトは、ストックホルムの図書館でのリサーチから始まることもある。何時間もかけ、15キロにもおよぶ本からかき集めたテキストとイメージが好奇心に満ちた色に塗られたデザイン、物語へと形を変える。Byggstudio は、自分たちでプロジェクトを考案することもある。たとえば、Vintage Plant という

プロジェクトでは「中古」の観葉植物と、それらひとつひとつの背景にある物語を集めている。Hanna と Sofia は、2006年にコペンハーゲンにあるデンマークデザイン学校のビジュアルコミュニケーションのMFA を取得している。

Daniël Maarleveld
ダニヘル・マーレフェルト
http://www.danielmaarleveld.nl/

Daniël Maarleveld was born in Amsterdam, the Netherlands, in 1981. Thanks to his father, who practised calligraphy, he developed an interest in typography at an early age. He studied multimedia design (1999-2003) at the Grafish Lyceum in Utrecht (NL) and graphic design at the Gerrit Rietveld Academy in Amsterdam (2003-07). His degree projects included the PenJet (a printer that prints with an pen) and the Akidenz diploma (a typeface shaped by a computer script). In both of these projects, techniques shape a new graphic vocabulary. Daniël Maarleveld has been working as a free-lance graphic designer since 2005.

1981年、オランダのアムステルダムに生まれる。カリグラフィーの仕事をしていた父親のおかげで、幼少の頃からタイポグラフィに興味をもっていた。ユトレヒトの Grafish Lyceum でマルチメディアデザイン（1999年〜2003年）、またアムステルダムの Gerrit Rietveld Academy でグラフィックデザイン（2003年〜07年）を習得した。彼の卒業制作は、PenJet（ペンを使って印刷するプリンター）と Akidenz diploma（コンピュータースクリプトの形をしたタイプフェイス）である。それらのプロジェクトによりテクノロジーが新しいグラフィック言語が形作った。2005年よりフリーランスのグラフィクデザイナーとして活動している。

Deanne Cheuk
ディアンヌ・チューク
http://www.deannecheuk.com/

Deanne Cheuk is a New York-based art director, illustrator and artist from Perth, Western Australia. Cheuk has art directed or designed numerous publications, including Tokion Magazine. Cheuk's art direction has been heavily influenced by her illustrative work and she is renowned for her illustrative typography. She has been

commissioned by top international companies, including American Express, Dell, Lane Crawford, Levi's, Nike, Converse, Sprint, Swatch, Target, MTV, Gap, Urban Outfitters, The Guardian, T Magazine and The New York Times Magazine. She has worked with David Carson, Doug Aitken and Conan O'Brien. In 2005, Cheuk released her first book, Mushroom Girls Virus - which sold out worldwide immediately. She has also judged competitions for the Art Director's Club NY and the Type Director's Club NY, and from 2008-2010 was on the Board of the American Institute of Graphic Arts, AIGA/NY.

オーストラリア、パース出身、現在はニューヨークを拠点に活動するアートディレクター、イラストレーター、アーティスト。これまでに、Tokion Magazine を初めとする数々の出版物のアートディレクション、デザインを手がけてきた。彼女のアートディレクションは、自身のイラストの仕事から強い影響を受けており、彼女はイラストのタイポグラフィでも良く知られている。これまでに、American Express、Dell、Lane Crawford、Levi's、Nike、Converse、Sprint、Swatch、Target、MTV、Gap、Urban Outfitters、The Guardian、T Magazine、The New York Times Magazine などの世界的に名高い企業の仕事や、David Carson、Doug Aitken、Conan O'Brien の仕事を手がけてきた。2005年には『Mushroom Girls Virus』と題する初の作品集を出版し、すぐに売り切れになった。また、Art Director's Club NY や The Type Director's Club NY などのコンクールの審査員を務める。また、2008年から2010年には、American Institute of Graphic Arts, AIGA/NY の役員を務めた。

Edrem
エドレム
http://edrem.blogspot.com/

Edrem is a blog of drawings that started a few years ago. Three friends are sharing doodles that they describe as "quick black and white funny cool drawings", putting just an idea quickly on paper. Some drawings has been featured in Vice magazine, and since then, Edrem works on different project for brands such as April77, Marc by Marc Jacobs, or even Kesselskramer.

数年前に始まったドローイング

のブログサイト。「即興で描いたモノクロの楽しいドローイング」と表現するイラストを友人3人でシェアしている。彼らの作品はVice magazineで紹介され、それ以後、EdremとしてApril77、Marc by Marc Jacobs、Kesselskramerなどのブランドとさまざまなプロジェクトを行っている。

Eika (Eibatova Karina)
エイカ（エイバトーヴァ・カリーナ）
http://www.flickr.com/photos/eika_dopludo/

Eika (Eibatova Karina) is an illustrator and fine artist. Was born in Russia (USSR), Leningrad. Since young age was fond of drawing. Studied classical art disciplines in Saint-Petersburg, Fine Art education in Sweden and contemporary art in Moscow. Eika runs a creative collective called Dopludo. The main themes in her creativity are nature, infinite space, hair, organic shapes etc. The main tool is a simple pencil.

イラストレーター、ファインアーティスト。ロシアのレニングラード生まれ。幼少の頃から、ドローイングが好きだった。サンクトペテルブルクで古典芸術を、スウェーデンでファインアートを、モスクワで現代アートを学ぶ。彼女はDopludoという名のアート集団を率いている。彼女の創作の主要なテーマは、自然、無限空間、毛、有機的な空間などである。画材は主に鉛筆を使用している。

Ethan Park
イーサン・パーク
http://ethanyoungpark.blogspot.com/

"Ethan was a pleasure to work with, keeping to our deadlines, accommodating with our many sketch changes, and providing us with a number of options to pick from. His organic, smart and solid approach make his illustrations tangible, yet whimsical, fun, yet witty and all very much alive." Deputy AD, Fast Company
"Ethan is interested in the role of typography within communication and works across a range of media. He takes everyday objects such as food, clothing and natural forms as a starting point for experimental typography through which objects appear in unexpected locations, where the division between types and image is blurred."

「とても働きやすく、〆切も守り、度重なる変更にも柔軟に対応し、クライアントがたくさんの選択肢から選べるように数多くのアイデアを提出する。有機的で、機知に富んでいて、筋の通ったアプローチによって、彼のイラストは具体的で、しかもちょっと滑稽で、面白くて、ウィットに飛んでいて、さまざまな要素が共存しているような作品になっている」（Fast Company、アートディレクター）「彼は、幅広いメディアに渡るコミュニケーションや業務のタイポグラフィの役割に興味を持っている。食べ物、衣服、自然の形などの日常のモノを題材に、作品を文字とイメージの境界線を曖昧にさせるような想定外の場所に出現させるという実験的なタイポグラフィを作っている」

Evelin Kasikov
http://evelinkasikov.com/

Evelin Kasikov is a London based artist and designer who transforms printing processes into hand-embroidery. Originally from Estonia, she developed her love of craft during MA studies at Central St Martin's. Evelin's approach to craft is analytical, her labour-intensive handmade works are meticulously precise. Evelin's work has been featured in many design publications such as It's Nice That, Novum, Étapes and Computer Arts. Her unique CMYK cross-stitch technique has led to commissions from the likes of WIRED and The Guardian.

ロンドンを拠点に活動するアーティスト、デザイナー。通常、印刷で行う作業を、手刺繍で仕上げている。エストニア出身。セントラル・セントマーティンズ美術デザイン学校の修士課程でクラフトの魅力を知る。彼女のクラフトへのアプローチは分析的であり、重労働となる手作業は、きわめて細かく正確だ。これまでに、It's Nice That、Novum、Étapes、Computer Artsなど数々の出版物で作品が紹介されている。彼女のユニークなCMYKのクロススティッチは、WIREDやThe Guardianに掲載された。

G&V
ジー・アンド・ブイ
http://www.gandv.se/

Although originally born in the United States, Vassili Brault was raised in Paris where he studied photography and art-direction at the ESAG Penninghen School of Arts. He first worked as a photographer and art director after receiving his Master's of Fine Arts degree with Jury Honors. In 2007, Vassili moved to New York to become the new creative director of an international advertising agency focusing on brands in the luxury and up-scale market. After a few years he returned back to his roots as an independent, multidisciplinary visual artist and soon founded the G&V collective: a group of selected artists that share the same values: collaborating to produce exceptional work in film and photography among many other mediums that are visible in the realm of independent fashion and other luxury markets.

Vassili Braultはアメリカで生まれ、フランスのパリで育つ。パリのESAGペニンゲン高等専門学校で写真とアートディレクションを学ぶ。修士号の卒業制作で審査員賞を受賞した後、フォトグラファーとアートディレクターとして活動を開始。2007年、Vassiliはニューヨークに移り住み、ラグジュアリーと富裕層向けの市場を専門とする国際的な広告代理店のクリエイティブディレクターを務める。数年後、彼のルーツである、さまざまな手法を用いて表現するインディペンデントのヴィジュアルアーティストに転身。その後、同じ価値観を持つアーティストを集めたグループG&Vを設立。映像、写真、その他インディペンデントなファッションブランドやラグジュアリー市場のあらゆるヴィジュアル媒体の共同制作をしている。

hort
ホート
http://www.hort.org.uk/

Hort began its inhabitance back in 1994, under the previous stage name of Eike's Grafischer Hort. But who the hell is Eike? Eike is the creator of HORT. HORT - a direct translation of the studio's mission. Once a household name in the music industry. Now, a multi-disciplinary creative hub. When not designing Hort likes to involve themselves in various other activities like teaching, creative workshops and advising companies on strategy and brand management. Hort enjoys informing people creatively or in a way that makes information easier to understand; working for companies that are starting off and need some assistance in establishing themselves; illustrating a company's personality by developing a brand; creating a visual connection with music and it's listener; translating the artwork of an album beyond its sleeve. Our communication services are based on many years of international work for top brands and on our profound knowledge of contemporary art, culture, music and lifestyle.

EikeのGrafischer Hortを前身として1994年に設立。しかし、Eikeとは何者か？ Eikeは、HORTの創設者である。HORTとはスタジオの使命の直訳である。音楽業界の仕事を請け負った後、現在では様々な領域に渡るクリエイティブを手がけている。デザイン以外にも、講義、クリエイティブのワークショップ、企業への戦略やブランドマネージメントのコンサルタントを行っている。Hortは、人々へ創造的な方法で情報を伝達することを好み、そうすることによって、情報がより簡単に理解されると考える。会社設立の手助けを必要としている企業のために働き、ブランド力を発展させることによってその企業のオリジナリティを設計し、音楽と視聴者とを繋げるヴィジュアルを創造し、アルバムのアートワークをそのカバーデザインへと発展させる。Hortのコミュニケーションサービスは、長い期間におよび一流企業との国際的な仕事を手がけてきた経験や、現代アート、カルチャー、音楽、ライフスタイルの深い理解に基づいている。

Jonathan Zawada
ジョナサン・ザワダ
http://zawada.com.au/

Jonathan Zawada is an internationally renowned graphic designer and creative director who works across the music, publishing, fashion and corporate industries from his home in Sydney, Australia. Catching the collective eye of the design world with his album cover for The Presets' Blow Up in 2003, Jonathan has since created a breadth of work for clients including Modular Records, Surface to Air, Nike, BMW and Coca Cola. Jonathan has become best known for his varied approach to the discipline of design, his personal ventures (including the mathematical style guide, Fashematics), his projects as one third of "TRU$T FUN!" and his personal art exhibitions which have taken place in Australia and internationally.

Biography

国際的に知られるグラフィックデザイナー、クリエイティブディレクター。オーストラリアのシドニーを拠点とし、音楽、出版、ファッション、コーポレイトアイデンティティを手がけている。2003 年に発売された The Presets のアルバム『Blow Up』のカバーデザインを手がけたことで注目を集め、以来、Modular Records、Surface to Air、Nike、BMW、Coca Cola など幅広い領域の仕事に携わっている。Johonathan は、数学とファッションを題材としたウェブ『Fashematics』などの個人プロジェクト、彼の他 2 名と共に行っているプロジェクト『TRU$T FUN!』、国内外での展覧会など、デザインへの多様なアプローチで知られている。

Daijiro Ohara
大原大次郎
http://omomma.in/

A graphic designer. Born 1978. The core of Ohara's creativity activity is design work and motion image production that centers on typography with a high level of 'DIY-ness'. He also engages in various other kinds of self-initiated projects, including the publication of "MOZINE", a zine series centering on letters, the field work project "Moji Saishuu", as well as exhibitions and workshops.

グラフィックデザイナー。1978年神奈川県生まれ。DIY 性の高いタイポグラフィを基軸としたデザインワークや映像制作を中心に、文字のZINE シリーズ『MOZINE』の発行、フィールドワーク『文字採集』、展覧会、ワークショップなど、自発的なデザイン活動を展開する。

István Szugyiczky
イストヴァン・スージスキー
http://www.szugyiczky.com/

István Szugyiczky is a Hungarian graphic designer and illustrator living and working in Budapest. Having graduated at the Hungarian Academy of Fine Arts in 2001 with an MA in graphic design, he has since then worked for several design studios and agencies as senior designer and art director for clients like Microsoft, Cisco Systems, Aegon, Dresdner Bank, Korean Daewoo Bank, Volkswagen, Nikon, Adidas, Bacardi, Miller, Danone and Coca Cola. István also made posters for charity organizations like Greenpeace or Unicef and

featured in many social and environmental poster exhibitions all around the world. Working as an independent graphic designer since 2008, he is interested in illustrative typography, lettering, illustrations, identity design and posters. He is also running his own street wear label XENO.WS.

ブダペスト在住、ハンガリー人のグラフィックデザイナー、イラストレーター。2001 年にハンガリー芸術大学を卒業以来、数社のデザインオフィス、代理店でシニアデザイナ・アートディレクターを務め、Microsoft、Cisco Systems、Aegon、Dresdner Bank、Korean Daewoo Bank、Volkswagen、Nikon、Adidas、Bacardi、Miller、Danone、Coca Cola などのクライアントの仕事に携わる。また、Greenpeace や Unicef へのチャリティポスターも制作し、世界各地の社会、環境関連のポスター展で発表した。2008 年からはフリーランスのグラフィックデザイナーとして活動を開始し、イラストで描かれたタイポグラフィ、レタリング、イラスト、アイデンティティデザイン、ポスターなどの制作に力を入れている。また、自身が手がけるストリートウェアブランドXENO.WS も展開している。

Julien de repentigny
ジュリアン・デ・ルパンティニー
http://www.visualadvice.com/

Julien De Repentigny is a graphic designer from Montreal living in London. The work of this graduate of UQAM has been published in many magazines, books and blogs such as IDN Magazine, THE DESIGN AND DESIGN BOOK OF THE YEAR, TypePlayer, Computer Arts, Applied Arts, Esquire Magazine (Taiwan), Nightlife Magazine, grafika, enroute, etc. His work revolves mainly around type in graphic spaces and making complex set design environment. He uses different materials to express himself such as paper, acrylic and neon lights. His style can be defined as modern pop art with playful sleekness. Lately he has been working on installations combining web interactions and his usual set design style.

モントリオール出身、ロンドン在住のグラフィックデザイナー。ケベック大学モントリオール校の卒業制作は、IDN Magazine、THE DESIGN AND DESIGN BOOK OF THE YEAR、TypePlayer、Computer Arts、Applied Arts、Esquire

Magazine（台湾）、Nightlife Magazine、grafika、enroute など、さまざまな雑誌、本、ブログに紹介された。彼は、グラフィック空間、複雑なセットデザインにおけるタイポグラフィを主に手がけている。作品制作に用いる材料は、紙、アクリル、ネオンライトなどさまざまである。彼のスタイルは、現代ポップアート、遊びがあってなめらかなもの、と表現されるだろう。最近では、ウェブのインタラクションと彼の定番であるセットデザインを組み合わせたインスタレーションを制作している。

Julien Vallee
ジュリアン・ヴァレ
http://www.jvallee.com/

Julien Vallée is a Montreal based artist and designer working in a wide range of fields, such as art direction, motion graphics, print design, art installation as well as film and design for the television industry. Trying to explore the different fields of design, he's been questioning the relative roles of the computer and handmade processes in design. He tries to get in touch with every aspect of the environment, using manual processes strongly supported by the technological tools of today to bridge as many of these disciplines as he can. Through his plastic experimentations and projects for his clients such as the New York Times, AOL, Swatch and MTV, he tends to re-invest image synthesis technologies, mainly in mixing digital conception phase with fragile implementation material, such as paper and cardboard. Over the year, Julien's work was granted recognitions such as the Young Guns 6 Award of the Art Directors Club in New York and the Creative Review Award 2010 in London, UK. It was also largely published in a variety of graphic books and magazines around the world such as Advanced Photoshop, Eye, IdN and Tactile High-touch visuals as well as Tangible and Computer Arts for which he designed the cover illustration. Since 2008, Julien has been part of several exhibition such as YCN Live in UK, ADC YG6 in New York and Taiwan, Illustrative Festival in Zurich and at the Create Berlin gallery just to name a few. He's been lecturing in different part of the world for new media festivals such as Offf Paris, Flash On The Beach in the UK, Inspiration Fest in Buenos

Aires as well as in Seoul. He also conducted workshops in Sweden, Argentina and Canada.

モントリオールを拠点に、アートディレクション、映像、印刷物のデザイン、アートインスタレーション、テレビ業界の映像やデザインなど幅広い領域で活動するアーティスト、デザイナー。デザインのさまざまな領域を開拓すべく、デザインにおけるコンピューターと手作業の相互的役割を問い続けている。彼は、環境のあらゆる側面への接触を図るために、マニュアルな手法を今日のテクノロジーで支え、上記の諸領域の橋渡しを試みている。New York Times、AOL、Swatch、MTV などのクライアントのために制作したプラスティックを使った実験やプロジェクトを通して、デジタルで構想したものと紙やボール紙などの脆い実用的な素材を混合するなど、イメージを合成する技術を再投資しようとしている。Julien の活動は Young Guns 6 Award of the Art Directors Club（ニューヨーク）や the Creative Review Award 2010（ロンドン）広く知られるようになり、また、彼の作品は Advanced Photoshop、Eye、IdN、Tactile High-touch visuals、Tangible、表紙のイラストレーションを手がけた Computer Arts などのグラフィック関連の本や雑誌に掲載されている。2008 年より、YCN Live（イギリス）、ADC YG6（チューリッヒ、台湾）、Illustrative Festival（チューリッヒ）、Create Berlin gallery などの多数の展覧会に参加。また、Offf Paris、Flash On The Beach（イギリス）、Inspiration Fest（ブエノスアイレス）、Samwon Paper Gallery（ソウル）などのメディアフェスティバルでの講演や、スウェーデン、アルゼンチン、カナダでワークショップも行っている。

Kazuhide Abe
阿部一秀
http://www.kazuhideabe.com/

Abe became a freelance art director and graphic designer after working at Uchu Country and Hamada Jimusho. He handles printed material such as posters and editorial design as well as graphic design, with unique typography as a core competency. In 2004, he was awarded a prize at the Tokyo TDC Awards, and in 2009, he was nominated for another.

宇宙カントリー、浜田事務所を経て現在フリーランスのアートディレ

クター・グラフィックデザイナー。独自のタイポグラフィを軸に、ポスターやエディトリアルなどの印刷物やグラフィック制作をメインに活動。2004年、TOKYO TDC賞（一般部門）受賞。2009年、TOKYO TDC賞ノミネート。

Lesley Moore
レスリー・ムーア
http://www.lesley-moore.nl/

Lesley Moore is an Amsterdam-based graphic design agency, founded in May 2004 by Karin van den Brandt (1975, Blerick, The Netherlands) and Alex Clay (1974, Lørenskog, Norway). Van den Brandt and Clay studied at the Arnhem Academy of the Arts (The Netherlands). Current and recent clients include: BIS publishers, Centraal Museum Utrecht, Mark Magazine, MTV, De Volkskrant (Gorilla, in collaboration with Herman van Bostelen and De Designpolitie), Warmoesmarkt, Wilfried Lentz Art Gallery, Wolters Kluwer. Merits include: European Design Awards for best Magazine 2008, Official selection Chaumont 2008, European Design Awards Miscellaneous and Jury Award 2007, Art Directors Club Netherlands 2007 and Dutch Design Awards 2007.

アムステルダムを拠点としたグラフィックデザインエージェンシー。2004年4月、Karin van den Brandt（1975年生まれ。オランダのブレック出身）とAlex Clay（1974年。ノルウェーのローレンスクーグ出身）によって設立。Van den Brandt と Clay は、アーネム芸術アカデミー（オランダ）で学んだ。最近のクライアントは、BIS publishers、Centraal Museum Utrecht、Mark Magazine、MTV、De Volkskrant（Gorilla、Herman van Bostelen と De Designpolitie との共同制作）、Warmoesmarkt、Wilfried Lentz Art Gallery、Wolters Kluwer など。また、European Design Awards for best Magazine 2008、Official selection Chaumont 2008、European Design Awards Miscellaneous および Jury Award 2007、Art Directors Club Netherlands 2007、Dutch Design Awards 2007 など受賞歴多数。

Mario Hugo
マリオ・ヒューゴ
http://www.mariohugo.com/

Mario Hugo is a New York based artist and designer. Though he spends an inordinate amount of time in front of a computer, he still feels most honest with a pencil and two or more sheets of paper. Mario is a founder and creative director of the studio and artist management agency Hugo & Marie.

ニューヨークを拠点に活動するアーティスト、デザイナー。コンピューターの前で相当な時間を費やすが、最も素直に表現できるのは鉛筆と紙を使うことだと感じている。Marioは、スタジオとアーティストマネージメントエージェンシーHugo & Marieの設立者であり、クリエイティブディレクターでもある。

Mike Perry
マイク・ペリー
http://www.mikeperrystudio.com

Mike Perry works as a designer and artist working in a variety of mediums, including—but not limited to—books, magazines, newspapers, clothing, drawing, painting, and illustration, Mike Perry is compelled by the ways in which the hand-drawn informs and deepens contemporary visual culture. Perry works regularly for a number of editorial and commercial clients including Apple, The New York Times, Dwell, Target, Urban Outfitters, eMusic, and Nike. In 2004, he was chosen as one of Step magazine's 30 under 30, and, in 2007, as a "Groundbreaking Illustrator" by Computer Arts Projects. In 2008, he received Print magazine's New Visual Artist award and the ADC Young Guns 6. His work has been exhibited around the world including the recent, solo show, Lost in the Discovery of what Shapes the Mind, at the Minneapolis College of Art and Design in Minneapolis, MN. In addition to his commercial, non-profit, and art work, Perry has also published extensively. His first book, Hand Job, published by Princeton Architectural Press in 2006, focuses specifically on the relevance and beauty of hand-drawn type in the digital age. Over and Over: A Catalog of Hand-drawn Patterns (Fall 2008), explores the similarly nuanced texture, humor, and elegance of illustrative patterns. A third book, entitled Pulled: A Catalogue of Screen Printing, is out now. His self-published magazine, Untitled, explores a variety of themes both playful and lofty. The most recent issue, Untitled 5 was released Summer 2010.

書籍、雑誌、新聞、アパレル、ドローイグ、ペインティング、イラストなどさまざまなメディアを手がけるデザイナー、アーティスト。手描きや現代ヴィジュアルカルチャーの手法を用いている。Apple、The New York Times、Dwell、Target、Urban Outfitters、eMusic、Nikeなどのエディトリアルやコマーシャルのクライアントを持つ。また、2004年には、Step magazineの「30 under 30」、2007年には、Computer Arts Projectsの「Groundbreaking Illustrator」に選出された。2008年には Print magazine の New Visual Artist award、ADC Young Guns を受賞。また、最近ミネアポリス美術デザインカレッジで行われた個展『Lost in the Discovery of what Shapes the Mind』など、世界各地で展覧会を開催。さらに、商業的、商業的でないもの、純粋なアート作品に加え、自らが著者を務める書籍を発行している。最初の書籍は、2006年に Princeton Architectural Press 社から出版された『Hand Job』であり、デジタル時代における手描きの文字を扱った。2冊目となる2008年の『Over and Over: A Catalog of Hand-drawn Patterns』では、イラストで描かれた柄のテクスチャ、ユーモア、エレガンスを追求。3冊目『Pulled: A Catalogue of Screen Printing』は2011年発売。また、彼が自費出版で発行している雑誌『Untittled』は、遊び心溢れた完成度の高いさまざまなテーマを扱っている。5号目は2010年夏に発売。

Mina Tabei
田部井美奈
http://minatabei.com/

A graphic designer. Born 1977. A graduate of Musashino Art University Junior College of Art and Design. In 2003, Tabei joined the office of Kazunari Hattori, and in 2006, she also began doing independent work. Her works include "Tento" for PARCO Shibuya (2010), logo design for LIBRO de KVINA (2010), calendar design on "Nogawa Kasane Yama to Jikan" for the publisher Yama to Keikokusha (2010), tabloid design for the French Embassy's "No Man's Land" (2009), the publishing of an independent book "PANTIES" (2009), art direction for Ginza Kanematsu's catalogs (2009, 2010), graphic design for Mitsubishi Estate's "Marunouchi Art Salon Tokubetsuhen" (2008), and book design for "Rakuen ni Magari", for Kadokawa Publishing. In 2009, Tabei joined the atelier Kvina.

1977年生まれ。 武蔵野美術大学短期大学部卒業。2003年より有限会社服部一成に勤務。2006年より個人の仕事もスタート。主な仕事に、渋谷PARCO『Tento』（2010）LIBRO de KVINA（2010）などのロゴデザイン、山と渓谷社『野川かさね 山と時間』（2010）カレンダーデザイン、フランス大使館『No man's Land』（2009）タブロイドのデザイン、自主制作本『PANTIES』（2009）の出版、銀座かねまつ商品カタログ（2009、2010）のアートディレクション、三菱地所株式会社『丸の内アートサロン特別編』（2008）グラフィックデザイン、角川書店『楽園に間借り』（2007）ブックデザインなど。2009年アトリエ『Kvina』に参加。

nam
ナム
http://n-a-m.org/

NAM is a Tokyo-based graphic / art collective, formed in May 2006 by a graphic designer Takayuki Nakazawa and a photographer Hiroshi Manaka. Currently a team of more than 10 artists, NAM creates works with hints of fantasy, fusing graphic design point of view into photographic expression.

2006年5月グラフィックデザイナーの中沢貴之とフォトグラファーの間仲宇により、「日常とファンタジー」をテーマとした制作活動をスタートさせる。2007年、各ジャンルのアーティストたちの参加により総勢15名以上のグラフィックコレクティブとなる。

Niessen & de vries
ニーセン・ド・フリース
http://www.niessendevries.nl/

Esther de Vries and Richard Niessen have been working together since 2006. Together they share an interest in close collaborations with clients, striving to produce 'new' works. Instead of one straightforward concept, they seek longevity through richness in layers, they like to emphasize the materiality of the work and avoid references: each work generates it's own universe. Being graphic designers doesn't limit them to two dimensions or sole print work: their designs range from exhibitions to textiles and from ceramics to coins. Besides their work for clients they work on self-

Biography

work for clients they work on self-commissioned projects.

Esther de Vries と Richard Niessen は、2006 年より共に働いている。「新しい」作品を作るため、2人はクライアントとの親密な共同作業を積極的に行っている。ひとつの分かりやすいコンセプトではなく、何層にも重なり合い、長い間続くものを探し、参照を避け、具体的なものを強調する。それぞれの作品は、独自の世界を生成する。彼らにとってグラフィックデザイナーであることは、2次元や単なる印刷物に仕事を限定することにはならない。彼らは、展覧会からテキスタイルまで、陶器からコインまで、幅広いデザインを手がける。また、クライアントとの仕事以外にも、自分たちのプロジェクトも手がけている。

Norio Nakamura
中村至男
http://nakamuranorio.com/

Born 1976 in Kawasaki, Japan. After graduating from the College of Art at Nihon University, Nakamura joined Sony Music Entertainment, and then went in to establish his own studio (Nakamura Norio Seisakushitsu) in 1998. He has won awards from the Mainichi Advertisement Design Competition, the Tokyo ADC Awards, the Tokyo TDC Awards, a Silver Prize from the 76th NY ADCs, and an Excellence Prize from the Japan Media Arts Festival. His works include planning and art direction for the PlayStation video game "I.Q.", graphic design for the artists Maywa Denki, work done for the magazine Kokoku Hihyo, for "Tetopettenson" on the program Minna no Uta, and for his "Katte ni Kokoku" series.

1967 年川崎市生まれ、日本大学芸術学部卒業後 (株) ソニー・ミュージックエンタテインメントを経て、1998 年中村至男制作室を設立。毎日広告デザイン賞、76th NY ADC 銀賞、文化庁メディア芸術祭優秀賞、東京 ADC 賞、東京 TDC 賞など受賞。 代表的な仕事に、PlayStation『I.Q』の企画とアートディレクション、『明和電機』のグラフィックデザイン、雑誌「広告批評」、みんなのうた『テトペッテンソン』、『勝手に広告』など。

OK-RM
オーケー・アールエム
http://www.ok-rm.co.uk/

OK-RM is a design studio founded in 2008 by Oliver Knight and Rory McGrath. The practice encompasses a variety of activities that include visual identity, publication design, art direction, editorial and digital projects. In 2008 OK-RM initiated In Other Words, a series of projects which explore the complexities and intricacies of the English language. Their work has been featured in 20 under 30, New York, 2010; How Very Tokyo, Tokyo, 2009; Live Archive, New Museum, New York, 2009; Illustrativ, Zurich, 2008; Book Show, Eastside Projects, Birmingham, 2010; Design Marketo, Milan Design Fair, 2010 and published in Eye Magazine. OK-RM have participated in the following public talk events: Best British Books (A Proposal), London, 2010 and Typography Critiques, V&A, London, 2010. The studio has worked with a variety of artists and cultural organisations including Barbican Art Gallery, Hayward, Raking Leaves, Serpentine Gallery, Artangel, Wolfgang Tillmans and Snowdon.

2008 年に Oliver Knight と Rory McGrath によって設立されたデザインスタジオ。 ヴィジュアルアイデンティティ、出版物のデザイン、アートディレクション、エディトリアルとデジタルプロジェクトなど、様々な分野で活動している。2008 年には、英語という言語の複雑さや錯綜を開拓するプロジェクト『In Other Words』を始動。彼らの仕事は、in 20 under 30 (2010年、ニューヨーク)、How Very Tokyo (2009年、東京)、Live Archive - New Museum (2009年、ニューヨーク)、Illustrativ (2008年、チューリッヒ)、Book Show - Eastside Projects (2010年、バーミンガム)、Design Marketo - Milan Design Fair (2010年、ミラノ) で発表され、Eye Magazine に掲載された。 また、Best British Books: A Proposal (2010年、ロンドン) や Typography Critiques - V&A (2010年、ロンドン) で講演も行った。 また、Barbican Art Gallery、Hayward、Raking Leaves、Serpentine Gallery、Artangel、Wolfgang Tillmans、Snowdon などのさまざまなアーティストや文化機関の仕事を手がけている。

Pablo Alfieri
パブロ・アルフィエーリ
http://www.pabloalfieri.com/

Pablo Alfieri is a graphic designer an illustrator from Buenos Aires, Argentina. After working as an art director in local studio, he decided to create his own place, "Playful", where he dedicates all his passion for graphic design, illustration and typography. Characterized by a constant search of simplicity in geometrics shapes, a mix between analogous and digital, lead Pablo to captivate the interest of companies like Nike, MTV International and Latinamerica, Snickers, Chevrolet, Motorola and Nextel, agencies like W+K China, BBDO Poland, Mother Argentina, A&P London, Craverolanis, Mc Cann Erikson Argenitna. Recently his artworks were selected on books like "Stereographics" and "Flashback" from Victionary, "Design and Design '09" and "One Day" from Index Book, "Super Identity" from All Right Reserved and "Typography Today" from ArtPower, magazines like "Joia Magazine", "Computer Arts", "Digital Arts" and "Advanced Photoshop", and websites like "Fubiz", "NotCot", "Behance" and "CpLuv". Pablo joined with Gula's owner, Mariano Farias, (an experienced motion graphic designer) to created PLENTY, a new graphic and motion graphic design studio meant to be a reference in Argentina that has work with brands as MTV, Discovery Channel, Fox, Johnnie Walker, Chandon, among others.

アルゼンチンのブエノスアイレスを拠点に活動するグラフィックデザイナー。地元のデザイン会社でアートディレクターを務めた後、グラフィックデザイン、イラスト、タイポグラフィへの情熱をすべて注げる場所「Playful」を創立。アタログとデジタルの手法を用いて、幾何学の形を追求し続ける彼のスタイルは、Nike、MTV (インターナショナル、ラテンアメリカ)、Snickers、Chevrolet、Motorola and Nextel などの企業、W+K China、BBDO Poland、Mother Argentina、A&P London、Craverolanis、Mc Cann Erikson Argenitna などの代理店を魅了してきた。 また最近では、Victionary 社の『Stereographics』や『Flashback』、Index Book 社の『Design and Design '09』や『One Day』、All Right Reserved 社の『Super Identity』、ArtPower 社の『Typography Today』などの書籍、Joia Magazine、Computer Arts、Digital Arts、Advanced Photoshop などの雑誌、Fubiz、NotCot、Behance、CpLuv などのウェブサイトに作品が掲載された。Pablo は、Gula 社のオーナーである Mariano Farias (経験を積んだモーショングラフィックデザイナー) と共同

で、モーショングラフィックのデザインスタジオ PLENTY を設立し、MTV、Discovery Channel、Fox、Johnnie Walker、Chandon などの仕事を手がけている。

Sasha Prood
サーシャ・プルード
http://www.sashaprood.com/

Sasha Prood grew up just outside of Philadelphia, Pennsylviania and currently resides in Brooklyn, New York. She creates typography, illustrations, patterns and graphics using pencil, pen and watercolor with the computer. Thematically her works lean toward the organic, natural and scientific with vintage, utilitarian and childhood influences.

ペンシルベニア州のフィラデルフィア郊外で育ち、ニューヨークブルックリンに在住。鉛筆、ペン、水彩絵の具とコンピューターを用い、タイポグラフィ、イラストレーション、パターンを手がけている。 作品の底に流れるテーマとして、オーガニックなもの、自然、科学などがあり、その他にもヴィンテージ、機能性、そして幼少時代の記憶から影響を受け続けている。

Serial Cut™
シリアルカット
http://www.serialcut.com/

Serial Cut™ is a Madrid based studio, established in 1999 by Sergio del Puerto, working on a wide variety of worldwide projects, but focusing mainly on Art Direction. Serial Cut™ works alongside an ever-growing team of professionals, who specialize in different areas such as photography, design, motion-graphics and 3D design. Depending on the nature of a given project, different collaborators are chosen to give each piece a new dimension. Big and small companies from arts and culture, fashion or entertainment industries are our primary clients; for each new project from a given client, we like to change the look and feel of the design. Image and type are a great combination that we like to use on all the projects we work on. Typography plays an important role in the end product.

1999 年に Sergio del Puerto によって設立されたマドリッドを拠点にしたデザインスタジオ。主にアー

ディレクションに力を入れ、国内外で様々なプロジェクトを手がけている。Serial Cut™ は、写真、デザイン、映像、3Dデザインなど異なる分野で活躍するプロフェッショナルたちと共に働いている。プロジェクトの内容によって、適したコラボレーターが選ばれ、新しい次元の作品が仕上げられる。アート、カルチャー、ファッション、エンターテイメント業界の大小の企業が主なクライアントである。プロジェクトによって、提出するデザインのスタイルを変えている。どのプロジェクトにおいても、イメージと書体を組み合わせた手法を用いることを好んでいる。タイポグラフィは、最終的な製品において重要な役割を果たしている。

Thorbjørn Ankerstjerne
トロンボニスト・アンカースチャーネ
http://www.ankerstjerne.co.uk/

Danish Thorbjørn Ankerstjerne graduated in 2007 from Central Saint Martins with a BA in graphic Design. Ankerstjerne has lived in London for 8 years and is working as a freelance art director as well as the editor and art director of film, art and design publication FILE Magazine. Ankerstjerne works across a broad range of media from moving image, installations to conventional graphic design and his range of clients includes fashion brands, musicians to corporate institutions.

デンマーク人。2007年にセントラル・セントマーティンズ美術デザイン学校のグラフィックデザイン科を卒業。現在までにロンドンに8年間在住し、フリーランスのアートディレクターとして活動中。また、映画、アート、デザインの雑誌 FILE MAGAZINE のエディターおよびアートディレクターを務めている。映像、インスタレーション、グラフィックデザインなど幅広く手がけており、ファッションブランド、ミュージシャン、企業などをクライアントに持つ。

Tobias Battenberg
トラビス・バッテンベルク
http://www.tobias-battenberg.de/

Tobias Battenberg is a communication designer from Köln, Germany. He was born in Germany in 1982 and from 2004-2010 he studied communication design and sustainability at ECOSIGN, in Köln, Germany.

In 2010 his thesis was about "Sustainable-Communication" and he also won the "Kölner DESIGN Preis (Award)" and the "Froschkönig (Frog- king)" Award. In 2011 he started his own studio located in Köln, Germany. His composition designs are focused on sustainability and social responsibility.

Tobias Battenberg はケルン出身のコミュニケーションデザイナー。1982年にドイツで生まれた彼は、2004年から2010年にかけてコミュニケーションデザインとサステイナビリティー（持続可能性）についてECOSIGNデザイン学校にて学び、2010年にはサステイナブル・コミュニケーションを題材にした卒業作品がKölner DESIGN Preis 賞とFroshkönig 賞を受賞。翌2011年に自身のスタジオをケルンに設立し、サステイナビリティーと社会責任を体現する作品を創作し続けている。

Tobias Röttger
トビアス・ロートゲール
http://www.tobiasroettger.de/

"For a designer, the problem about getting older is not aging as such but rather the loss of curiosity – I remain curious." Tobias Röttger, born 1980 in Aachen, studied Communications Design at Mainz Design Academy and Swinburne University in Melbourne, Australia. The graphic designer and illustrator lives in Berlin, works for magazines, designs record covers and develops corporate design. Alongside his freelance work he is also a part of the graphic design office HORT. The multi-disciplinary design studio works internationally for large and small customers. Tobias Röttger is a member of this extraordinary office that sees itself as a place where you can and should learn. A place that draws inspiration from everyone and everything, is constantly in motion, constantly changing and expanding. As a member of this collective he is at once creative motor, drive belt and gear like everyone else in HORT. In this knowledge he constantly develops himself and his projects, which have already attracted national and international attention. Among other things, Tobias Röttger has won prizes from TDC Tokyo, ADC Europe and a Gold Medal from ADC Germany. Wallpaper Magazine selected him in 2008 as one of

the best graduates in the graphic design category. But in order to receive inspiration you must also give it to others and so he and Eike König have run various workshops, some with students from the Mainz University of the Applied Sciences and the Bauhaus University Weimar but also Berlin's University of the Arts.

「デザイナーとして、歳を取ることは問題ではないが、好奇心を失うことは問題である。私は強い好奇心を持ち続けたい。」Tobias は、1980年にオーストラリアのアバッチで生まれ、マインツデザインアカデミーとスィンバーン大学でコミュニケーションデザインを学ぶ。グラフィックデザイナー、イラストレーターとしてベルリンに移住し、雑誌、レコードカバーのデザインや企業デザインを手がける。フリーランス業以外にも、彼はグラフィックデザイン事務所HORTに所属している。HORT は、国内外の大小のクライアントのさまざまな仕事を請け負うデザインスタジオである。Tobias は、このスタジオを、自分の力が発揮でき、また多くのことを学べる場所だと考えている。ここでは、さまざまな人や事柄からインスピレーションを受け、常に前進し、変化し、規模が拡大している。この集団の一員として、彼はクリエイティブのモーター部分である。彼は常に自分自身と手がけるプロジェクトを開発し、それらは国内外で注目を集めている。さらに、Tobias は、TDC Tokyo、ADC Europe、ADC Germany（金賞）など多数の受賞をしている。2008年にはグラフィックデザイン分野において、最も期待される学生として、Wallpaper Magazine に掲載された。また、インスピレーションを受けるためには、自らもインスピレーションを他の人に与えることが大切だと考え、彼とEike König（HORT の設立者）は、マインツ大学応用科学研究所、ワイマール・バウハウス大学、ベルリン芸術大学などでワークショップを行っている。

Travis Stearns
トラヴィス・スターンズ
http://www.travisstearns.com/

Awhile ago I had this concept to brand myself as the World's Greatest Designer. My belief, like many who have followed this line of thought, was that if I said it then maybe people would actually believe it. Of course, working hard does help the idea as well. As of late, my work has been greatly inspired by contemporary art, particularly digital art. I've had the

esteemed pleasure to share my work with Nylon Magazine, Wired Magazine, Mass Appeal, AIGA Minnesota, IAmSound Records, Swindle Magazine, Ghostly International, and Nixon Watches to name but a few. In 2008, I was selected as one of Print Magazine's 20 New Visual Artists of the Year.

すこし前に、私は自分自身を「世界で最も優れたデザイナー」と定義付けた。こういった考え方をする多くの人と同じように、私が信じていることは、口に出してしまえば人も信じるのではないだろうか。もちろん、これを実現するためには、熱心に働かなければならないのだが。最近、私の作品は、現代アート、特にデジタルアートにインスパイアされている。これまでに、Nylon Magazine、Wired Magazine、Mass Appeal、AIGA Minnesota、IAmSound Records、Swindle Magazine、Ghostly International、Nixon Watches などに作品を提供している。2008年には、Print Magazineの20人の若手ヴィジュアルアーティストの一人として選出された。

Wonder Wonder
ワンダーワンダー
http://cargocollective.com/

Wonder Wonder is the Brooklyn-based creative studio of Hikaru Furuhashi. Hikaru works in the areas of graphic design, branding, illustration, surface design and editorial projects. She draws inspiration from her youth in the northern Japanese Alps and her passion for non-western folk and pop art in envisioning her meticulous designs. Wonder Wonder's work has been featured in publications such as 3D Typography, 1,000 More Greetings, Brooklyn Diary and ReadyMade.

ブルックリンを拠点にした古橋ひかるのデザインスタジオ。ひかるは、グラフィックデザイン、ブランディング、イラストレーション、表層材デザイン、出版物のプロジェクトなどを手がける。特有の綿密なデザインを構想するにあたって、北日本アルプスで過ごした幼少時代の記憶、また、非西洋圏のフォーク／ポップアートに対する情熱をインスピレーションの源とする。Wonder Wonder の手がけた作品は、3D Typography、1,000 More Greetings、Brooklyn Diary、ReadyMade に掲載された。

タイポグラッフィクス　プレイ＆ワーク

タイポグラフィの現在進行形

2011年6月30日　初版第1刷発行

カバーデザイン　北山雅和（HELP!）
本文デザイン　庄野祐輔

編集　庄野祐輔・藤田夏海・吉田知哉
翻訳　藤田夏海・内山隆太郎・徐周煥・廣瀬剛

発行人　籔内康一
発行所　株式会社ビー・エヌ・エヌ新社
　　　　〒150-0022
　　　　東京都渋谷区恵比寿南一丁目20番6号
　　　　fax. 03-5725-1511
　　　　e-mail. info@bnn.co.jp

印刷・製本　シナノ印刷株式会社

© 2011　BNN, Inc.
ISBN 978-4-86100-770-5
Printed in Japan